NEW AND OLD PRAYERS

AND READINGS

For the High Holy Days, Shabbat, and Festive Occasions

Edited and Compiled by

Dov Peretz Elkins

© 2000 Dov Peretz Elkins

ISBN 0-918834-21-X
Library of Congress Catalog Card Number 99-091832
Printed by Lithoid Printing Corp., East Brunswick, NJ
Printed in the United States of America

This book is printed on recycled paper. A portion of the profits will go to MAZON: The Jewish Response to Hunger. Readers are invited to make their own contributions to:

MAZON
12401 Wilshire Blvd.,
Los Angeles, CA 90025
(310) 442-0020

For a complete catalog of books contact:

Growth Associates Publishers
212 Stuart Road East
Princeton, NJ 08540-1946
609/497-7375
E-mail: DPE@DPElkins.com
www.DPElkins.com

Rabbi Shimon taught:
Make not your prayers routine.

Pirke Avot 2:18

Rabbi Elazar would recite a new prayer every day.
Rabbi Abahu recited a new blessing each day.

Talmud Yerushalmi, Berakhot 4:3

One sigh uttered in prayer is of more help
than all the choirs.

Shmuel Yosef Agnon, Nobel Laureate

More things are wrought by prayer
than this world dreams of.

Alfred, Lord Tennyson

NEW AND OLD PRAYERS AND READINGS
For the High Holy Days, Shabbat, and Festive Occasions

Edited by Rabbi Dov Peretz Elkins

TABLE OF CONTENTS

ACCEPTANCE

Inclusiveness and broad understanding in the sphere of ideas is encouraged by a pure heart that is bereft of evil intent. Such an understanding will not dampen holy feelings of passion of a pious person. Just the opposite. Understanding broadens the bedrock of the fervor of dedication to God.

Acceptance and understanding are armed with a deep trust that God lives in all living beings. Even when we experience injurious and negative actions, there must still be found deep inside a vital illumination of sanctity. This sanctity is found even within the appearance of evil, even among those sick with heresy and devoured with doubts. When we recognize the corps goodness and sanctity, a great tolerance and acceptance is born, which surrounds all with the cord of compassion. "I will gather you all together, O people of Yaakov" (Micah 2:12).

A higher sanctity overflows with love, compassion, acceptance and understanding, as its most luminous hallmark. Meanness, rigidity and anger stem from neglecting God, and the dimming of the flame of holiness. The greater one's search for the Almighty in one's heart, the greater will be that one's love of all God's creatures. An understanding and accepting person will love the wicked and the doubters, and wish to bring them closer to God, standing as a shining example of faith.

By our very nature we demonstrate our love of others to those in whom we find traits of goodness. In this way we find goodness all around us. Thus are we protected from harmful people when we wish to share our love.

To find the corps of goodness in others we sometimes need to labor and seek strongly. At times this may mean sinking to the deep, dark territories for the sake of finding the true goodness which is the basis of all, the true light of all life.

Often we need to break into the chaos of the universe to find its goodness. When we reach the highest level of divine-like perfection, we see the basic unity of all life, and its diversity of approaches.

When an individual boasts of being the possessor of the sole truth, declaring that I alone am ruler, there can be no harmony. We must diligently strive to achieve the enlightened amity of God's desire. This emerges not by suppressing any power or idea, but rather by encompassing all of them into the vast sea of infinite light, where all of God's creation finds its unity, where every person is brought high, every creature is lifted up, and everyone is sanctified.

Rabbi Avraham Yitzhak HaKohen Kook
(Translated and adapted by Rabbi Dov Peretz Elkins)

***

JUDAISM CONDEMNS PREJUDICE

Judaism teaches the value of *adam yahid*, the Mishnaic concept of one human being created originally so that no one can say, "My parent was greater than your parent."

Judaism teaches the value of ahavat ha-briot, love for all God's created beings, the principle that entails acting in a loving fashion to any and all human beings.

Judaism teaches the value of *bakesh shalom ve-rodefehu*, to seek peace and pursue it, the obligation to actively reduce conflicts. There are a series of laws and ethical teachings advocating peace, conflict resolution, methodologies in prohibiting violence against the innocent.

Judaism teaches the value of hesed and rahamim, compassion, especially for those who are disadvantaged or vulnerable.

Judaism teaches the value of *darkhei shalom*, the ways of peace. There are many Talmudic rulings on preserving societal peace, including inter ethnic relations, such as feeding the poor of the gentile for the sake of the ways of peace.

Judaism teaches the value of ger, stranger. There are a series of laws governing love of strangers, empathy with foreigners, and the insistence on the inclusion of strangers in every aspect of society.

Judaism teaches the value of *hakem takim imo*, a law designed to encourage us to aid anyone in distress.

Judaism teaches the value of tzedek tzedek tirdof, the absolute obligation to pursue justice, the obligation to actively promote justice in all of life's endeavors.

Judaism teaches the value of *tzelem Elohim*: Judaism teaches that every human being is made in the spiritual image of God. It doesn't matter what we look like, how smart we are, or what we do for a living -- we are all made unique and deserving of respect.

Judaism teaches the value of umot ha-olam, the nations of the world. That we must care for and respect everyone, especially the ill, the aged and vulnerable.

Rabbi Julie K. Gordon and Rabbi Jonathan Ginsburg

***

2

FROM THE KABBALAH

"The pomegranates are in bloom" - this refers to the young children who pore over Torah, who sit for hours; they are like the seeds of pomegranates. (Midrash, *Shir HaShirim Rabba* 6:11).

Rabbi Shimon ben Lakish declared: "Even the most unobservant Jew is as full of mitzvot and good deeds as a pomegranate is with seeds." (Midrash, *Yalkut Shimoni* on *Shir HaShirim* 4:3).

The Talmud queries: "How is it possible that the famous scholar and teacher, Rabbi Meir, studied with his master, Elisha ben Abuya, even after Elihsa became an agnostic?" "Our teacher discovered a pomegranate. He enjoyed the essence, and discarded the rind" (Talmud, *Hagiga* 15b).

In the same way, when you eat a pomegranate, keep in mind that you are affirming every kind of Jew, no matter what background or level of observance.

When a Jew finds good things about another Jew, even those who forget the Torah and are distant from God, it is favorable to accept them unconditionally. Why? Because every Jew is as full of good deeds as a pomegranate.

This is the true and deeper meaning of the teaching of the Talmudic sage: "He enjoyed the essence, and discarded the rind." It is proper for an accepting and open-minded Jew to seek out the good points of other Jews, and to cast aside the rind.

One can enjoy the goodness and overlook the thoughts and acts with which one does not accept. When one sees only the good in other Jewish souls, the other parts are not noticed, and hence ignored.

Adapted from Rabbi Eliezer Shlomo Schick,
Rosh Hashanah L'Ilanot (Jerusalem: Hasiday Breslov)

***

GOD SIGHED A GREAT SIGH OF HOPE

Rabbi Yerachmiel gathered the children of the village to him.

"Listen, children, listen. For a great mystery is about to be revealed to you.

"In the beginning, God made a single human from the dust of the earth. This one was red, yellow, brown, black, and white, for all the sands of creation were used to fashion it. Male and female, it was, for God had not yet separated the sexes. And God said: This one is in My Image, for this one includes all creation in one being.

"God had thought this being would be happy, but it was not happy. It was lonely. So God divided the one human in two, female and male. And then these two divided themselves even further until the unity of the first person was lost in the divisions created by the many people who followed.

"And God was saddened by the false divisions. So God called all the people together and stood them in a great valley. God called each person to stand before a divine mirror in which each person saw reflected not her own image, but the images of everyone else.

"Many people were frightened by the strange mirror, and ran away to hide. But others understood that God was reminding them of their unity. And these people set for themselves a great task: to help each of us see the whole world reflected in each face. God helped them. God took the great mirror and made millions upon millions of tiny mirrors. God placed these tiny mirrors in the eyes of every human being, even you and me, so that if you look in another's eyes you will see reflected there the whole world and the One who created it.

"You are the children of those daring few, and it is time for you to carry on their work: to learn to look into the eyes of another and see the whole world and the One from Whom the whole World flows. If You fail, if you see only yourself reflected in God's mirror, the lie you will live will burn the world to a cinder. The whole world is waiting for you, my children. You must see the truth and proclaim it. You must open your eyes and see."

And the children looked at each other in awe. Some saw and smiled. Some saw and cried. Some could not see at all. But all held tight, one to the other, and God sighed a great sigh of hope.

Rabbi Rami M. Shapiro

***

AL HET: THE POWER OF THE TONGUE

Death and life are in the power of the tongue (Proverbs 18:21).

Rabbi Shimon ben Gamliel said to his servant, "Go out and bring me a good sort of food from the market place." He went out and brought him tongue. He said, "Go out and get me a bad sort of food from the market place." He went out and brought him tongue. Rabbi Shimon ben Gamliel said, "Why is it that when I asked you for something bad you brought me tongue again?" The servant answered, "From it, the tongue, comes good and bad. When the tongue is good there is nothing better than it; when bad, there is no evil worse." (Midrash, Vayikra Rabbah).

"You shall not go up and down as a tale bearer among your people; neither shall you stand idly by when the blood of your neighbor is spilt. I am the Lord" (Leviticus 19:16).

It is forbidden to make a derogatory comment about a person, even if it is true
(Hafetz Haim 1:1).

Any comment, even if it is not derogatory, that might ultimately cause financial loss, physical pain, mental anguish or any damage, is considered evil speech and is forbidden (Maimonides).

Any method of conveying derogatory information about others is forbidden: writing, hand or finger motions and facial expressions (Hafetz Haim 1:8).

Once there were two people sitting in a rowboat. One suddenly started making a hole on his side of the boat. The other screamed. The first countered and said, "What do you care what I do on my side of the boat?" (Midrash, Leviticus Rabbah)

Why does the Torah teach us there was one person created in the beginning? For the sake of peace among people, that one might say to another, "My parent was greater than yours." The sages also taught, "For the sake of the different families, that they might not quarrel with one another." Now, if at present though originally but one person was created they quarrel anyway, how much more would they have quarreled had two been created? (Babylonian Talmud, Tractate Sanhedrin)

Rabbi Jonathan Ginsburg and Rabbi Leslie K. Gordon

***

THE PARADOX OF OUR TIME

The paradox of our time in history is that we have taller buildings, but shorter tempers; wider freeways, but narrower viewpoints; we spend more, but have less; we buy more, but enjoy it less. We have bigger houses and smaller families; more conveniences, but less time; we have more degrees, but less sense; more knowledge, but less judgment; more experts, but more problems; more medicine, but less wellness. We have multiplied our possessions, but reduced our values.

We talk too much, love too seldom, and hate too often. We've learned how to make a living, but not a life; we've added years to life, not life to years. We've been all the way to the moon and back, but have trouble crossing the street to meet the new neighbor. We've conquered outer space, but not inner space; we've cleaned up the air, but polluted the soul; we've split the atom, but not our prejudice.

We have higher incomes, but lower morals; we've become long on quantity, but short on quality. These are the times of tall people, and short character; steep profits, and shallow relationships. These are the times of world peace, but domestic warfare; more leisure, but less fun; more kinds of food, but less nutrition. These are days of two incomes, but more divorce, of fancier houses, but broken homes. It is a time when there is much in the show window and nothing in the stockroom; a time when technology can bring this letter to you, and a time when you can choose either to make a difference or just hit delete."

Student at Littleton High School, Colorado, after students were killed by crazed murderer

*****

FOR THOUGHTS, WORDS AND WORKS...

All that we ought to have thought and have not thought,
All that we ought to have said, and have not said,

All that we ought to have done, and have not done.
All that we ought not to have thought, yet have thought,

All that we ought not to have spoken, and yet have spoken,
All that we ought not to have done, and yet have done.

For thoughts, words, and works,
pray we, O God, for forgiveness.

Persian Prayer
*****

AL HET FOR THE SHOAH:
A CALL TO REPENTANCE

For the sin which we committed before You and before them by closing our ears.

> *And for the sin which we committed before You and before them by not using our power.*

For the sin which we committed before You and before them by being overcautious.

> *And for the sin which we committed before You and before them by hesitating.*

For the sin which we committed before You and before them by treachery toward sisters and brothers.

> *And for the sin which we committed before You and before them by being content with those times.*

For the sin which we committed before You and before them by fearing the powerful.

> *And for the sin which we committed before You and before them by bowing to their will.*

For the sin which we committed before You and before them by continued frivolity.

> *And for the sin which we committed before You and before them by rationalization.*

For the sin which we committed before You and before them by our silence.

> *And for the sin which we committed before You and before them by our words of prejudice.*

For the sin we committed against You and before them by making your cross a sign of hatred rather than a sign of love.

> *For all these sins, O God of forgiveness.*
> *Forgive us, pardon us, and grant us strength to say 'Never Again."*

From "A Christian Service in Memory of the Holocaust" in *Liturgies on the Holocaust: An Interfaith Anthology*, ed. Marcia Sachs Littell and Sharon Weissman Gutman

***

AL HET

On the Jewish High Holy Days we take collective responsibility for our lives and for the activities of the community of which we are a part.

Although we realize that we did not create the world into which we are born, we nevertheless have responsibility for what it is like as long as we participate in it.

While the struggle to change ourselves and our world may be long and painful, it is our struggle. No one else can do it for us. To the extent that we have failed to do all that we could to make ourselves or our community all that we ought to be, we ask God and each other for forgiveness-and we now commit ourselves to acting differently this coming year.

Ve-al kulam, Elohah selihot, selah lanu, mehal lanu, kaper lanu.
For all our sins, may the Force that makes forgiveness possible forgive us, pardon us, and make atonement possible.

For the sins we have committed before you and in our communities by being so preoccupied with ourselves that we ignore the larger problems of the world in which we live;

And for the sins we have committed by being so directed toward outward realities that we have ignored our spiritual development;

For the sins of accepting the current distribution of wealth and power as unchangeable;

And for the sins of giving up on social change and focusing exclusively on personal advancement and success;

For the sins of feeling so powerless when we hear about oppression that we finally close our ears;

And for the sins of dulling our outrage at the continuation of poverty, oppression, and violence in this world;

And for the sins we have committed by allowing our food and our air to be poisoned;

For the sins of not doing enough to save the environment;

And for the sins of not doing enough to challenge sexist institutions and practices;

And for the sins of turning our backs on—or participating in—the oppression of gays and lesbians;

And for the sins of not doing enough to alleviate homelessness, poverty, and world hunger;

For the sins of allowing media indoctrination to convince us that others are motivated solely by money, power, or narrow self-interest;

And for the sins of not recognizing the deprivation of meaning—and the systematic frustration of our need for mutual recognition, love, and spiritual nourishment—as the source of so much frustration and pain in our society;

8

For the sin of accepting a world in which the "bottom line" is money and power, and not fighting for a new bottom line of love and caring;
And for the sin of being cynical about the possibility of building a world based on love;
And for the sin of spreading negative stories about people we know;
And for the sin of listening and allowing others to spread negative stories;
For the sin of not publicly defending our leaders when they are unfairly attacked, and for the sin of not giving our leaders, rabbis, educators, artists, and child caregivers, the emotional and material support they need to continue to do the work that we depend on them to do;
For these sins we ask God and each other to give us the strength to forgive ourselves and each other.
For the sins we have committed by not forgiving our parents for the wrongs they committed when we were children;
And for the sins of having too little compassion or too little respect for our parents or for our children;
For the sins of cooperating with self destructive behavior in others or in ourselves;
And for the sins of not supporting each other as we attempt to change;
For the sins of not seeing the spark of divinity within each person we encounter or within ourselves:
And for the sins of not learning from and giving adequate respect and care to our elders and to our teachers:
For the sins of being jealous and trying to possess and control those whom we love;
And for the sins of being judgmental of others and ourselves;
For the sins of withholding love and support ;
And for the sins of doubting our ability to love and get love from others;
For the sins of insisting that everything we do have a payoff;
For the sins of not recognizing the beauty within ourselves;
And for the sins of not recognizing the beauty that surrounds us;
For the sins of not allowing ourselves to play;
And for the sins of being manipulative or hurting others to protect our own egos;

Ve-al kulam, Elohah selihot, selah lanu, mehal lanu, kaper lanu.

For the sins we have committed by not publicly supporting the Jewish people and Israel when they are being treated or criticized unfairly;
And for the sins we have committed by not publicly criticizing Israel or the Jewish people when they are acting in opposition to the highest principles of the Jewish tradition:

9

For the sins of not recognizing the humanity and suffering of the Palestinian people and the injustice they face living under the unwanted occupation;

And for the sins of punishing the entire Palestinian people for the terrorist acts of a small number;

For the sins of allowing conservative or insensitive leaders to speak on behalf of all American Jews, and allowing our institutions to be governed by those with the most money rather than those with the most spiritual and ethical sensitivity;

And for the sins of not supporting those institutions and leaders that have attempted to provide alternative voices;

For the sins of being critical of Jewish life from a distance rather than from a personal involvement or commitment;

And for the sins of not spending more time engaged in learning the Jewish tradition and studying Jewish history literature, and holy texts;

For the sins of giving up on Judaism because it didn't satisfy our highest spiritual and ethical values, rather than engaging in the process of spiritually renewing our tradition;

And for the sins of allowing the spiritual renewers to divorce spirituality from the struggle for social justice and ecological sanity;

For the sins of acting as though Jewish pain is worse than everyone else's pain;

And for the sins of being insensitive or insulting to non-Jews;

For the sin of not recognizing and treating with respect the diversity of ethnic and cultural backgrounds, including Sephardic, Mizrahi, Ethiopian, Ashkenazic and Black Jews, the diversity of class backgrounds, the diversity of sexual orientation, and the diversity of ways that we address the spiritual truths of the universe;

For the sins of not having compassion for one another;

And for not taking care of one another;

For the sins of not sharing responsibility for childrearing;

And for the sins of self-absorption, allowing us to be insulated from the loneliness and needs of people around us;

For the sins of focusing only on our sins and not our strengths and beauty;

And for the sins of not adequately rejoicing and celebrating the beauty and grandeur of God's creation;

Ve-al kulam, Elohah selihot, selah lanu, mehal lanu, kaper lanu.

For all these, Lord of Forgiveness, forgive us, pardon us, grant us atonement.

***

Composed by Rabbi Michael Lerner, editor, *Tikkun* magazine, for Yom Kippur 5760, September, 1999

***

10

ATONEMENT

Yom Kippur punctuates our lives
Like a semi-colon,
Forboding a full stop--
Tomorrow, or year, from now.

   Has it been a year?
   Are we where we were before?
   Have we failed again?

But yesterday it seems, we stood before You.
Errors and sins we humbly acknowledged,
Numbly and dumbly we admitted our faults.

   Yesterdays are many; tomorrows, now, fewer.
   The children have grown and learned.
   But for ourselves, opportunities have passed.

And now we face Your judgment,
We can bear it, God, because of Your great mercy.
"You know how we are made;
You remember we are dust."

   But if last year we hoped
   For transformation,
   Then it's time to judge ourselves.

Your judgment we can bear;
It is our own that frightens us,
No punishment is greater, Lord,
Than what we give ourselves.

   Help us to forgive ourselves
   For having failed again.
   Arm us against self-hatred.
   Remove our bitterness of spirit.

We know that we shall sin again-
If life is granted--
We shall sin and we shall fail ourselves.

   We shall doubt you-
   And ourselves.
   We know the world will turn again,
   Still unredeemed,
   To meet next year's Yom Kippur.

11

Keep us from despair,
For that is the fatal sin.

Help us to forgive ourselves.
Send us healing.

Repentance was in Your plan from the beginning.
We know that we have sinned.
Help us know not only
What we have not done
But what we have the power to do.

Give us the faith, Lord.
Give us the will.

Rabbi Michael Hecht

***

CAN YOU FORGIVE?

We pray to You, Lord, today:

Not just to forgive us;
Because You have told us
That You can forgive only those things,
Which we have committed against You.

Can You forgive what we do to others?
Can You forgive what we do
To our sons and daughters?
Can You forgive what we do
To our future?
Can You forgive what we do
To ourselves?

We pray to You, this day:
To unsettle us,
To make us genuine,
To make us serious,
To make us concerned,
To make us responsive and responsible,
To make us change:

So that others will be able to forget,
So that our children will be able to forgive,
So that we will be able to forgive ourselves.

So that we will be able to feel
The wonderful sense of At-one-ment.

Rabbi Noah Golinkin

***

CLOSING PRAYERS

May you live to see your World fulfilled,
May your destiny be for worlds still to come;
May you trust in generations past and yet to be;
May you live to see your World fulfilled.

May your eyes shine with the light of holy words,
And your face reflect the brightness of the heavens.
May your lips ever speak wisdom,
Your fulfillment be in justice,
Even as you ever yearn to listen to the words of the
Holy Ancient One of Old.

May you live to see your World fulfilled,
May your destiny be for worlds still to come;
May you trust in generations past and yet to be;
May you live to see your World fulfilled.

May your heart be filled with intuition,
And your words be filled with insight.
May songs of praise be upon your tongue,
Your vision straight before you,
Even as you ever yearn to listen to the words of the
Holy Ancient One of Old.

May you live to see your World,
May you live to see your World fulfilled!

Original Text: Masekhet Brakhot 17a
Translation: Rabbi Lawrence Kushner

***

God be in my head,
And in my understanding;
God be in my eyes,
And in my looking;
God be in my mouth,
And in my speaking;
God be in my heart,
And in my thinking;
God be at my end,
And in my departing.

Sarum Missal
***

14

Glorious Lord, I give You greeting!
Let the plain and the hillside praise You.

Let the dark and the daylight praise You.
Abraham, founder of the faith, praised You:
Let the life everlasting praise You.

Let the birds and honeybees praise You,
Let the shorn stems and the shoots praise You.

Both Aaron and Moses praised You:
Let the male and the female praise You,

Let the seven days and the stars praise You,
Let the air and the ether praise You,

Let the books and the letters praise You,
Let the fish in the swift streams praise You,

Let the thought and the action praise You,
Let the sand-grains and the earth-clods praise You,

Let all the good that's performed praise You.
And I shall praise You, Lord of glory:
Glorious Lord, I give You greeting!

Gaelic Benediction

***

15

May the blessing of light be on you, light without and light within.

*May the blessed sunlight shine upon you and warm your heart
till it glows like a great peat fire,*

so that the stranger may come and warm herself at it, and also a
friend.

*And may the light shine out of the eyes of you,
like a candle set in the windows of a house,
bidding the wanderer to come in out of the storm.*

And may the blessing of the rain be on you—the soft, sweet rain.
May it fall upon your spirit so that all the little flowers may spring up,
and shed their sweetness on the air.

*And may the blessing of the great rains be on you,
may they beat upon your spirit and wash it fair and clean,*

and leave there many a shining pool where the blue of heaven shines,
and sometimes a star.

*And may the blessing of the earth be on you—the great round earth;
may you ever have a kindly greeting for them you pass
as you're going along the roads.*

May the earth be soft under you when you rest out upon it,
tired at the end of a day,
and may it rest easy over you when, at last, you lie out under it.

*May it rest so lightly over you that your soul may be off from under
it quickly,
and up and off, and on its way to God.*

And now may the Lord bless you, and bless you kindly.

Old Irish Blessing, *Reader's Digest*, January, 1967

***

[For Shabbat or Havdalah, substitute the word "week" for "year;" for Shabbat M'varkhim substitute "month" for "year;" for Shalosh Regalim substitute "season" for "year."]

May it be Your will, Eternal our God and God of all generations, that this New Year (week, month, season) will be for us, for all Israel, and for all people, a time of life.

Congregation: A year of life.
Leader: A year of peace.
Congregation: A year of peace.
Leader: A year of gladness.
Congregation: A year of gladness.
Leader: A year of joy.
Congregation: A year of joy.
Leader: A year of redemption.

Congregation: A year of redemption.
Leader: A year of hope.
Congregation: A year of hope.
Leader: And let us say: AMEN!

High Holy Day Family Service for Rosh Hashanah,
Stephen S. Wise Temple, Los Angeles

***

17

ENVIRONMENT

TITHE IT ALL, YES ALL

(Adaptation of Deuteronomy 14:22-23)

"You are to tithe, yes, tithe, all the produce of your seed-sowing, of what comes forth from the field, year after year ...."

Tithe all the fruit of your labors, income, energies, skills, knowledge.

Tithe for My orphaned species whose mother-forests have been chopped down, the isolated stands of Dogwood, the ancient Redwood.

Tithe for My widowed sea bird who can no longer find her nest.

Tithe for My impoverished earth – poisoned, stripped, scarred, dishonored.

Tithe for My impoverished children suffering with asthma who are forced to breathe foul air.

Tithe for the sake of My future tenants.

Tithe it all, yes all, to preserve the field from which it came.

Tithe by working your compost pile, and then watch My amazing worms squiggle in action.

Tithe it by surprising Me with yet greater mileage in your vehicles, that I may kvell in your ingenuity.

Tithe by bicycling or taking the train to work, and then notice My trees swaying in the wind.

Tithe it by bragging about the post consumer content of your paper, rather than its cranberry or pumpkin color.

Tithe by using less, by doing with less.

Tithe it all, "in order that you may learn to hold the Eternal, your God, in awe, all the days."

Barak Gale
Chair of Bay COEJL (Coalition on the Environment in Jewish Life)

***

GOD'S TERRITORY

The Almighty was seated on the Heavenly throne surrounded by the celestial hosts.
God remembered Avraham's demand for justice; Honi's insistence that it rain;
and even the evenings when Levi Yitzhak of Berditchev took God to trial.

But these were giants—what troubled God were the small, petty mean complaints directed against the Creator.

The Almighty summoned a messenger and bade him take this message to God's children on earth:

"Oh my children," it began, "for eons I have been listening to your complaints, in silence and with forbearance.

Now, in all fairness, listen to mine.
My children, I have given you sparkling lakes and shimmering rivers,
but you, because of thoughtlessness and greed, have polluted them,
so that children can no longer swim in them
and fish can no longer survive in their natural habitat.

*I have given you beautiful mountains and verdant valleys pleasing to the eye and soul,
but you have defiled them by erecting unsightly billboards on them and thus trampling my courts.*

I have bestowed upon you clear, clean air with which to fill your lungs,
but you seem to prefer the smoke that belches from your human-made factories,
incinerators, cars and cigarettes, which fairly obliterates the skies.

*I have given you a mind to seek truth,
and I confess at times you have used it well.
But now you are employing it as well as your billions to invade My territory
when you could well be expending your genius and substance to finding
cures for cancer, heart disease and a thousand other ailments...."*

Rabbi Jacob Polish

***

19

EARTH TEACH ME

Earth teach me stillness
as the grasses are stilled with light.

Earth teach me suffering
as old stones suffer with memory.

Earth teach me humility
as blossoms are humble with beginning.

Earth teach me caring
as the mother who secures her young.

Earth teach me courage
as the tree which stands all alone.

Earth teach me limitation
as the ant which crawls on the ground.

Earth teach me freedom
as the eagle which soars in the sky.

Earth teach me resignation
as the leaves which die in the fall.

Earth teach me regeneration
as the seed which rises in the spring.

Earth teach me to forget myself
as melted snow forgets its life.

Earth teach me to remember kindness
as dry fields weep with rain.

Ute Prayer

***

When I walk through your woods, O God, may my right foot and
my left foot
be harmless to the little creatures that move in its grasses, as our
Scripture teaches:
"They shall not hurt nor destroy in all my holy mountain." (Isaiah
65:25)

Talmud

***

20

O SPIRIT

O Our Father the Sky, hear us
and make us bold.

*O Our Mother the Earth, hear us
and give us support.*

O Spirit of the East,
send us your Wisdom.

*O Spirit of the South,
may we walk your path of life.*

O Spirit of the West,
may we always be ready for the long journey.

*O Spirit of the North, purify us
with your cleansing winds.*

Sioux Prayer
***

GOD'S WORLD

O world, I cannot hold thee close enough!
Thy winds, thy wide grey skies!
Thy mists, that roll and rise!

*Thy woods, this autumn day, that ache and sag
And all but cry with colour! That gaunt crag
To crush! To lift the lean of that black bluff!*

World, World, I cannot get thee close enough!
Long have I known a glory in it all,
But never knew I this:
Here such a passion is

*As stretcheth me apart,—Lord, I do fear
Thou'st made the world too beautiful this year;
My soul is all but out of me,—let fall
No burning leaf, prithee, let no bird call.*

Edna St. Vincent Millay
***

WE RETURN THANKS...

We return thanks to our mother,
the earth, which sustains us.

We return thanks to the rivers and streams,
which supply us with water.

We return thanks to all herbs,
which furnish medicines for the cure to our diseases.

We return thanks to the bushes and trees,
which provide us with fruit.

We return thanks to the wind,
which, moving in the air, has banished diseases.

We return thanks to the moon and stars,
which have given us their light,

We return thanks to the sun,
that has looked upon the earth with a kind eye.

Lastly, we return thanks to the Great Spirit,
in whom is found all goodness,
and who directs all things
for the good of God's creatures.

Iroquois Prayer

***

FAITH

THIRTEEN PRINCIPLES - I BELIEVE

Each one who aligns oneself every day with these principles of the faith and lives according to them can be assured that she/he will have a role in the World to Come for us and for all the peoples on the entire world soon.

1. May it be the Divine will that I believe with perfect faith in the G-d who is infinite and the blessed light that issues from that Infinite Source, Who is beyond time and space, yet Who longs to have a dwelling place among those in the worlds here below; and Who, out of loving beneficence to Her creatures, contracted Her light and Her radiant glory, in order to emanate, to create, to form, and to effectuate all that exists in the universe.

2. May it be the Divine will that I believe with perfect faith in the Oneness of G-d and of all creation, a oneness of the kind of One that has no second; and that all which exists in the universe exists solely according to the will of that G-d, who constantly calls everything into existence at every moment.

3. May it be the Divine will that I believe with perfect faith that the Creator has an intent and a purpose in creation. And that one of the aspects of that purpose is so that He shall become known to us by and through it; and that we creatures have a task to broaden and enlarge that knowledge/awareness until the world will be as filled with knowledge of G-d as the waters cover the sea.

4. May it be the Divine will that I believe with perfect faith that the hoped-for goal is that all of us will come to constitute one united/interconnected and organic whole and that every living being will know that You are the One who constantly causes its existence.

5. May it be the Divine will that I believe with perfect faith that all the pathways through which the Holy Spirit is manifest and revealed are of one piece with the Torah that was given at Sinai.

6. May it be the Divine will that I believe with perfect faith in the mission of Judaism. Which is one of the vital organs of the collective being that comprises all existence, and that through G-d's compassion on all creatures, it is revealed to them also their integral indispensability to all existence, how indispensable and integral they are to the health of all the species of the planet.

23

7. May it be the Divine will that I believe with perfect faith that the universe is not unaccounted for/abandoned and that every one who does good with his/her life fixes /takes part in the fixing of the world and vice versa /that every one who uses his/her life for evil participates in the destruction of the world; and that every action has an impact on the rest of existence.

8. May it be the Divine will that I believe with perfect faith that the amount of good in the world is greater than the amount of evil, and that the entire order of movement through the chain of evolution is designed to bring about the fulfillment of the Divine intention.

9. May it be the Divine will that I believe with perfect faith that the deeds of the fathers and mothers inure to the benefit of the children. and that the tradition that is passed on contains within it the seeds of the light of redemption.

10. May it be the Divine will that I believe with perfect faith that our prayers are heard and answered.

11. May it be the Divine will that I believe with perfect faith that the Holy Shechinah dwells within our midst and that all who show kindness to living creatures show kindness too to the Shechinah, and vice versa.

12. May it be the Divine will that I believe with perfect faith that physical death does not terminate the existence of the soul; rather, that there are innumerable worlds within which they return to live again.

13. May it be the Divine will that I believe with perfect faith in the fixing of the world/concept that the world can be fixed and its enlivenment; and that besides coming to life, the world will come to possess a consciousness and feeling, and as such will become a fitting vessel for the revelation of the Divine will.

Rabbi Zalman Schachter-Shalomi

FREEDOM

The experiences of camp life show that one does
have a choice of action.

*There were enough examples, often of a heroic
nature, which proved that apathy could be
overcome, irritability suppressed.*

We can preserve a vestige of spiritual freedom, of
independence of mind,
even in such terrible conditions of psychic stress.

*We who lived in concentration camps can remember
[those] who walked
through the huts comforting others, giving away
their last piece of bread.*

They may have been few in number, but they offer
sufficient proof
that everything can be taken from [someone] but
one thing:

*the last of the human freedoms– to choose one's
attitude
in any given set of circumstances, to choose one's
own way.*

Viktor Frankl

***

Merciful God - Have mercy upon your people in
countries where our people are still
victims of oppression (including....)

*Bless them with courage and fortitude in their
determination to live freely as Jews,
and to leave the land of their oppression.*

Strengthen our resolve to stand in solidarity with
them, to strive for their deliverance,
and to struggle for their freedom.

*Help us to understand that as we dedicate our
efforts for their redemption,
we also redeem ourselves.*

The battle for their survival assures our survival.
The uncompromising fight
for their rights raises our sense of purpose,
uplifts our lives,
and gives noble meaning to our existence.

*May Redemption and Freedom come speedily to our
beleaguered brothers and sisters.
May they be restored to the people, nation, and
destiny of Israel.*

May the prophetic promise be fulfilled in our time:
"For I shall redeem you from afar and your children
from the land of their captivity.
And Israel shall dwell in peace and security,
with none will make them afraid."

***

WE BELIEVE

We believe - that the world is beautiful and worth singing about.

We believe - that the world is good and is worth shouting about.

We believe - that the world is full of kindness and of faith
and that behind the facade is a design, profound and wonderful.

*We believe - that the success of evildoers, of bigots and tyrants –
is only temporary.
That the righteous will strike deep roots
and will grow in stature and in power.*

They will grow in the esteem and the admiration of humanity
like the stately palm tree and like the mighty cedar.

*We believe - that being Jewish means being godly;
that being godly means being just.*

We believe - that this is our goal and our destiny.
And to achieve our goal, our ancestors made a Covenant with God.

*We are glad to be the Children of the Covenant.
We will keep faith with our Covenant.*

We believe - that God loves freedom
and that God upholds champions of freedom.

*We believe - that the life of the Jew has been a struggle for freedom;
that the triumph of freedom is a most wondrous Miracle;
and that the survival of the Jew is a Miracle of Miracles.*

We believe - that God made a Covenant with our ancestors at Sinai:
never to forget Pharaoh and never to forget God;

*And to remember at all times and at all places
God's greatest claim on our loyalty:
"I am the Lord your God Who took you out of the land of Egypt,
out of the House of Bondage."*

We believe - that as Children of the Covenant
We are commanded to remember God, and never to forget Pharaoh.

Rabbi Noah Golinkin
***

GOD

WHERE IS GOD?

God is in the faith
By which we overcome the fear
Of loneliness, of helplessness,
Of failure and of death.

God is in the hope
Which, like a shaft of light,
Cleaves the dark abyss
Of depression, suffering, and despair.

God is in the love
Which creates, protects, forgives.

God's is the Spirit
Which broods upon the chaos
We have wrought,
Disturbing its static wrongs,
And stirring into life,
The formless beginnings,
Of the new and better world.

Adapted from Rabbi Mordecai M. Kaplan

***

GOD IN EVERY OBJECT

I hear and behold God in every object,
yet understand God not in the least,

Nor do I understand who there can be more wonderful than myself.
Why should I wish to see God better than this day?

I see something of God each hour of the twenty-four,
and each moment then,

In the faces of men and women I see God,
and in my own face in the glass,

I find letters from God dropped in the street—
and every one is signed by God's name,

And I leave them where they are,
for I know that others will punctually come forever and ever.

Walt Whitman

***

All is change in the realm of senses,
But unchanging is the Supreme Lord of Love.

Meditate on God, be immersed in God,
Wake up from your dream of apartness.

Know God and all chains break away.
No longer identify yourself with your body,
transcend birth and death.

All your desires will be fulfilled in God,
for God is One, there is none else.

Know God to be consecrated in your heart always,
Surely there is no more to know in life.

Contemplate and know that
the world is filled with God's presence.

Upanishads
***

THE LORD IS IN ME

The Lord is in me, the Lord is in you,
as life is in every seed.

O servant! Put false pride away, and seek for him within you.
A million suns are ablaze with light,

The sea of blue spreads in the sky,
The fever of life is stilled,

and all stains are washed away
When I sit in the midst of that world.

Hark to the unstruck bells and drums! Take your delight in love!

Rains pour down without water,
and the rivers are streams of light.

One love it is that pervades the whole world,
few there are who know it fully:

They are blind who hope to see it by the light of reason,

that reason which is the cause of separation –
The House of Reason is very far away!

Kabir - 15th century Indian mystic -
Translated by Rabindranath Tagore, *One Hundred Poems of Kabir*
(London: Macmillan & Co. Ltd., 1967)

***

GOD IS COMING TOWARD ME

Adonai, where shall I find You?
Your abode is hidden, very high.
Adonai, where shall I not find You?
Your Appearance permeates time and space
I seek Your closeness
With my full heart I cry out to You.
When I go toward You, I find you coming toward me!

Yehudah HaLevi

***

GOD - THE DIVINE ORIGINAL

In an age of copiers, computers and calculators there is only one original:

God is the original by whose standards we measure ourselves.

God is the unique being by Whose standards we judge ourselves.

As God is just, so we are commanded to be just.

As God is merciful, so we are commanded to be merciful.

As God is forgiving, so we are commanded to be forgiving.

May we be blessed with the talent to fulfill
the commandment to imitate our God - the Divine Original.

Rabbi Sylvan D. Kamens

***

OUT OF THE MOUTHS OF BABES

Who Is God?

The world is God's dollhouse, and we're His dolls.
He presses buttons and makes us talk and walk. *Elana, age 5*

I think he's a swarm of colors that creates life on this planet, *Martin, age 10*

God is a beautiful lady in a beautiful white dress. She sits in heaven with Her dress spread all around. It covers the earth and protects us. *Tracy, age 5*

God lives in the world and in the Temple, which is His house. When the blue light is on over the Ark where the Torahs are, that means He's home. *Richard, age 4*

He takes care of me. He's basically like my parents, but He's one person. I mean, my parents take care of me, but God takes care of them, and without God I wouldn't have parents. *Avishai, age 10*

Mommy, When Will the Lord Be Two? A Child's Eye View of Being Jewish Today
Ruth Seligman and Jonathan Mark (Kensington Publishers)

***

AWE AND MYSTERY

The tangent to the curve of human experience lies beyond the limits of
language.
The world of things we perceive is but a veil.
Its flutter is music, its ornament science,
but what it conceals is inscrutable.
Its silence remains unbroken; no words can carry it away.

Sometimes we wish the world could cry
and tell us about that which made it pregnant with fear-filled grandeur.
Sometimes we wish our own heart would speak of that which made it
heavy with wonder.

Out of the world comes a behest to instill into the air a rapturous song
for God,
to incarnate in stones a message of humble beauty,
and to instill a prayer for goodness in the hearts of all....

To meditative minds the ineffable is cryptic, inarticulate:
dots, marks of secret meaning, scattered hints, to be gathered,
deciphered and formed into evidence; while in moments of insight
the ineffable is a metaphor in a forgotten mother tongue.

The great yearning that sweeps eternity is a yearning to praise...
to serve.
And when the waves of that yearning swell in our souls
all the barriers are pushed aside:

the crust of callousness, the hysteria of vanity, the orgies of arrogance.
For it is not the I that trembles alone,
it is not a stir out of my soul,
but an eternal flutter that sweeps us all.

Rabbi Abraham Joshua Heschel

***

DU, DU, DU

Du, Du, Du!
You! You! You!

I sing to You!
Du, Du, Du!
Where do I find You?
Where do I not find You?

Wherever I go: Du! Where I am: Du!
Only You - None but You - Always Du!

Ay - You, You, You!
Ay - Du, Du, Du, Du!

When all is well: Du!
When problems come: Du!
Ay - You, You, You!
Ay - Du, Du, Du, Du!

In the East: Du! In the West: Du!
In the North: Du! In the South: Du!

Ay - You, You, You!
Ay - Du, Du, Du, Du!

Toward the sky: Du! Toward the Earth: Du!
Way above: Du!   Down below: Du!

Ay - You, You, You!
Ay - Du, Du, Du, Du!

Turn this way and that way: Only You!
I stay right here: Du, Du, Du Du!

Reb Levi Yitzhak of Berditchev

***

GRATITUDE

THANK YOU, GOD

Thank you, God,
For evening after day,
And for dawn after night.

*Thank You for changing times
And passing seasons.*

Each sunset is a sign for us;
Each summer's passing, a reminder;
Each year's end, a milepost.

*Thank You for seasons in life.
Thank You for joy.
Thank You for the pains of growth.
Thank You for the urgency that's caused by death.*

We are not stones that never change.
We are not ageless, immune, boring.

*A thousand years in Your sight are like a day.
For us a day is like a thousand years.*

Thank You that we can read the skies
And say, Another day has passed,
Another year—
so much to tell.

*Thank you for the challenges of being human,
That tomorrow is not repetitious of today.
Thank You that this moment is so precious.*

(Inspired by the first blessing before Sh'ma)

Rabbi Michael Hecht

***

TO BE THANKFUL FOR LIFE

Let me do my work each day;
and if the darkened hours of despair overcome me,
may I not forget the strength that comforted me
in the desolation of other times.

May I still remember the bright hours that found me
walking over the silent hills of my childhood,

or dreaming on the margin of the quiet river,
when light glowed within me,
and I promised my early God to have courage
amid the tempests of the changing years.

Spare me from bitterness
and from the sharp passions of unguarded emotions.

Lift my eyes from the earth, and let me not forget the uses of the stars.

Forbid that I should judge others lest I condemn myself.

Let me not follow the clamor of the world,
but walk calmly in my path.

And though age and infirmity overtake me,
and I come not within sight of the caste of my dreams,

Teach me still to be thankful for life,
and for times's golden memories
that are good and sweet;

and may the evening's twilight find me gentle still.

Max Ehrmann

***

THINK AND THANK

Thank God for the ability to see.

To see the rainbow, the change of seasons,
the beauty of paintings and sculpture.

Thank God for the ability to hear,

The babbling of brooks, the music of performers,
the voices of loved ones.

Thank God for the ability to taste.

*The wine of **kiddush**, the variety of spices,*
a hot drink on a cold day, a cold drink on a hot day.

Thank God for the ability to touch,

The alternating smoothness and hardness of rocks,
the pliant reed, the grain of the wood,
and your hand in mine.

Thank God for the ability to smell,

The fragrance of flowers and perfumes,
*the tantalizing aromas of food, the spices of **havdalah**.*

Thank God for the ability to think,

New ideas, the capacity to wonder, to have self-awareness.

Thank God for the ability to feel,

Compassion for those who hurt,
concern for those who are in need,
love for those who are dear to us.

Rabbi Bernard S. Raskas

***

GUIDED MEDITATIONS - Rosh Hashanah

[the dots.....indicate places the leader/reader might pause for people to sit quietly in meditation.]

****

Tekiah!

To some the shofar's blast brings a sense of awe, and excitement. To others its call brings a smile of joy, while still others hear the plaintive notes and respond with tears of longing for distant times or severed relationships. The horn delivers a different sound for each of us, but its call is universal. Awake! Awake your slumbering soul! Remember and pay attention to that which is Holy in your life.

Each of us is like a shofar--without the Divine breath which passes through us we would sit mute, empty. At the same time, each of us has the power to be our own Ba'al Tekiah--to carry the sound of the shofar in our minds and in our hearts, and to hearken to its voice within us.

Every time we hear the shofar it is both old and new, familiar and strange. So in a moment I will ask you, in like fashion, to experience something that is at once familiar and perhaps a bit strange as well.

The ruah, which is the wind, the spirit, that passes through the ram's horn, provides for every listener a link between a physical sound and the Divine presence. Likewise, each breath we take can connect our physical bodies with our spiritual existence. So I will ask you to pay attention to that spiritual link--to pay attention to your breath....

****

I invite you all to be sure that you are sitting comfortably for the next few minutes, and I invite you to shut your eyes. Take a deep breath. Hold it. And let it out. Again--deep breath...and let it out.

Now let's breathe normally and focus our awareness on the simple coming and going of our breathing....Simply pay attention to your breath as your chest rises and falls, or as you feel air enter and exit through your nose....You will naturally sense some distractions--such as noises inside or outside this sanctuary, or the normal chatter of your mind—whatever distractions you feel, neither resist them nor cling to them—just recognize them and then gently, effortlessly return your awareness back to your breath ....With each breath, breathe in a greater sense of peace...breathe in a greater sense of holiness... breathe in a greater sense of connection to the energy that unites the Universe.........

37

I invite you all to be sure that you are sitting comfortably for the next few minutes, and I invite you to shut your eyes. Take a deep breath. Hold it. And let it out. Again--deep breath...and let it out. Now let's breathe normally and focus our awareness on the simple coming and going of our breathing....Simply pay attention to your breath as your chest rises and falls, or as you feel air enter and exit through your nose....You will naturally sense some distractions--such as noises inside or outside this sanctuary, or the normal chatter of your mind—whatever distractions you feel, neither resist them nor cling to them—just recognize them and then gently, effortlessly return your awareness back to your breath....With each breath, breathe in a greater sense of peace...breathe in a greater sense of holiness...breathe in a greater sense of connection to the energy that unites the Universe...........

Now bring into your awareness the sound of the shofar. Recall a time when you listened to the shofar's voice, when you heard it's piecing cry, it's haunting call stirring your soul............

In a moment I will recite the names of the four shofar calls. In the silent spaces between these words listen within your heart for the sound of the shofar, hear its call and pay attention to its message--however it speaks to you. And when we get to the last call, the mighty sound of Tekiah G'dolah, you'll listen to it and then slowly, when you're ready, you'll open your eyes feeling relaxed, refreshed, and revitalized.

The first call, a single blast, is a symbol of wholeness, it reminds us that to be complete we must be spiritually awake -- in your heart, listen to Tekiah....

The next two calls comprised of many little notes symbolize how fragmented our lives can become.

The second call, is a series of three short calls each with a low note and a high note, reminding us to pay attention to everything, to honor everyone --big or small, high or low-listen to Sh'varim....

The third call, a series of rapid notes, an alarm reminding us of the urgency of time, reminding us to value every moment -- listen to T'ruah....

We close with a great single blast again--through our call to conscience--making Teshuvah, we return to wholeness. The final call is given with all the Ba'al Tekiah's strength, reminding us to hold nothing back, in order to give and receive the full and complete blessing of life -- listen within to Tekiah G'dolah....

...and now, very slowly, when you're ready, open your eyes, feeling relaxed, at peace, at one.

GUIDED MEDITATIONS - Yom Kippur

Our journey of the past year has brought us once again to the Gates of Repentance. Every day every step of the journey provides the opportunity for teshuvah. Every sunset and every dawn provides the opportunity for a fresh start. Yet through the wisdom of the ages we have created this special day.

By paying attention to the patterns of Nature the magical rhythms of change in the heavens and on earth we have maintained awareness of the cycles of the sun and moon and the seasons.

We mark this new season - in which we come together as a community in which we unite - not to raise a louder voice to God - but to bring nurturing and understanding to one another, to bring encouragement to share the frailties as well as the strengths of being members of the human family.

Some of our strength comes from our relationships to one another. Some comes from relationship with the Divine - evident in the world around and beyond ourselves, but present also within each of us - we have on Yom Kippur our greatest opportunity to open the gates that would otherwise restrain us.

In the midst of a day of abstinence and penitence - on a day when we may feel physically and mentally depleted, we may also have a greater opportunity to pay attention to and to connect to the Divine Source.

We sit quietly.... very quietly.... still even more quietly.... paying attention to our breath....our breath sustains us connects us to life, to all of Nature, to all that is beautiful . Our breath connects us to the wind that covers the corners of the earth. Our breath connects us to the breath of God.

We feel the quiet rhythm of our hearts sending nourishment to all the cells of our bodies, beating with a pulse which reverberates throughout the Universe - a vibration that co-mingles the energies of all that exists - of all that is Holy in the midst of this fast - this day of long meditation - there may be many distractions. The chatter of others - or of our own minds - natural discomfort or resistance that we may feel. We simply recognize all of this - softly paying attention to it. We note it - we name it - we accept it - and then gently - we detach from it - returning easily, effortlessly - to these words of meditation - or to the quiet awareness of our breath....

Let us now open gates within us - to deeply explore - the depths of this Holy Day. Let us surrender to the totality of the Universe - to its darkest depths - as well as to its magnificent brilliance. Let us feel ourselves opening fully to what is.

While for each of us that will be different - still we are all touched by the same eternal forces.

In the midst of this Day of Atonement - let us feel the openness of becoming at one - with ourselves. Let us feel the openness of becoming at one with our fellow human beings. Let us feel the openness of becoming at one - with the Source of all existence.

We sit in this stillness, and we open all gates that would otherwise bar us from achieving the greatness that is our Divine gift to receive.

We open the gates of our minds to new thoughts - to new ways of perceiving the perspectives of others and to ideas that may never before have been considered.

We open ourselves to new worlds of possibility as we open the gates of our minds.... feel the openness ... ... We open the gates of our bodies - with acceptance and love of what we are in flesh and blood and bone. We open our awareness to the miracle of our very existence; to the responsibility we have to care for ourselves - to continually renew the strength poured into our cells and organs by Divine blessing.

We open ourselves to a life of health and physical vigor - by opening the gates of our bodies. Feel the openness ... ...

We open the gates of our hearts with love and forgiveness - for ourselves - embracing ourselves for all that we are as well as for all that we are not, knowing that our self love will support all that we aspire to become. And that we must love and forgive ourselves - before we can truly love and forgive others.

We open ourselves to embrace all humanity, as we open the gates of our hearts.... Feel the openness ... ...

We open the gates of our souls - allowing, despite our doubts - the possibility of a Divine force which unites the Universe. We live the Sh'ma - by listening carefully - as strugglers in Israel - to the voice deep within us - that echoes Unity.

We open ourselves to the infinite richness of the Universe - by opening the gates of our souls. Feel the openness ....

We open these gates to receive the fullness of life - in our minds - in our bodies, in our hearts, and in our souls   We open these gates - and any others - which will lead us to greater fulfillment as God's creatures - which will open paths to living our true destinies on this planet - which will allow us to move in bliss and to bring along all who would share this path with us - our families, our friends, our neighbors, our fellow workers - all who we meet and touch.

We open all these gates - and enter a Divine garden - filled with light and music - sweet fragrances - gentle breezes - a garden of God's love, where each stepping stone accepts our gentle tread with the full support of the Universe.

And as we take these steps on this spiritual journey we experience the joy and fulfillment of knowing that we are moving with the love of Adonai - and that we can return to the Garden, and that we can walk on this Path - each and every day of our lives.

***

VISUALIZATION

Hear your Father, your King, the Creator and Sustainer of the entire universe, saying to you: I have given you the ability to create mental visualizations. Use My gift to elevate yourself. If there is a character trait that you need to improve, mentally visualize yourself doing so successfully. If you have a specific fault you need to overcome, visualize yourself overcoming that fault. If you wish to master a positive habit, visualize yourself mastering that habit. If you wish to reach high spiritual levels, keep visualizing yourself reaching that level. Be patient when you visualize. Be prepared to visualize yourself as you wish to be over and over again. Elevated visualizations elevate your whole being.

Rabbi Zelig Pliskin, *My Father My King*
(Mesorah Publications, Ltd., 1997)

***

A GUIDED IMEDITATION FOR SH'MA AND OTHER PRAYERS OF UNITY

[Leader reads slowly and paced. Participants may close their eyes, and be relaxed. Ed.]

Beloved God,
Show me the truth about this.
I now surrender all fears, doubts, and judgments,
and invite the light of perfect consciousness
to illuminate my path.

Pure love is present here and now, as God lives
in every person I meet.
I send love and appreciation to all my associates,
knowing with perfect confidence that he or she
is guided by the same Great Spirit that guides me.

I am not separate from my brothers and sisters,
but one with them.
I trust that my highest good is unfolding before me,
and I accept the very best that love and life have to offer.

I am worthy of living in the kingdom of Heaven [Malkhut Shamayim],
even as I walk the earth. I claim it now.
Thank you, God, for loving me infinitely,
and opening all doors for the highest good of all concerned.
I receive your love, and magnify it.

And so it is.

Alan Cohen

***

MEDITATION FOR OPENING OR CLOSING PRAYER

Lord of the springtime, Father of flower, field and fruit,
smile on us in these earnest days when the work is heavy and the toil
wearisome;
lift up our hearts O God, to the things worthwhile–
summer and night, the dripping rain, the song of the birds,
books and music, and the voices of our friends.

Lift up our hearts to these this night, and grant us Thy peace. Amen.

W.E.B. Du Bois

***

OVERCOMING OUR FAULTS AND FAILURES:
A Guided Imagery Exercise

A Jerusalem kabbalist, Colette Aboulker-Muscat, specializes in the use
of imagery in spiritual practice. The following guided imagery exercise
is based on her teaching.

Leader (slowly and paced): Close your eyes and imagine that a
beautiful apple tree is before you. There is a ladder leaning against the
tree. Go up the ladder. There are apples on the tree. Take one. Look
at it in your hand and see that it grows in size. Then it opens. Notice
inside any dark spots. These are your faults and failings– anger, pride,
whatever they are. Pluck them out with your other hand and throw
them away. The apple closes. It reduces to its usual size. You put it
back on the tree. You descend the ladder. Open your eyes.

Yitzhak Buxbaum

***

HEALTH AND HEALING

THE GOLDEN GLOW OF SUNLIGHT

After a long illness, I was permitted for the first time to step out-of-doors. And as I crossed the threshold sunlight greeted me.

As long as I live, I shall never forget that moment....
The sky overhead was very blue, very clear, and very, very high.

A faint wind blew from off the western plains,
cool and yet somehow tinged with warmth–like a dry, chilled wine.

And everywhere in the firmament above me,
in the great vault between the earth and sky,
on the pavements, the buildings–the golden glow of sunlight.

It touched me, too, with friendship, with warmth, with blessing.

And as I basked in its glory there ran through my mind
those wonderful words of the prophet:
"For you who revere My name the sun of righteousness shall rise
with healing on its wings" (Malachi 3:20).

In that instant I look about me to see whether anyone else
showed on their face the joy, almost the beatitude, I felt.

But no, there they walked–men and women and children,
in the glory of the golden flood,

and so far as I could detect,
there was none to give it heed.
And then I remembered how often I, too, had been indifferent to the
sunlight,
how often, preoccupied with petty and sometimes mean concerns,
I had disregarded it.

And I said to myself: How precious is the sunlight but alas,
how careless of it we are.

Rabbi Milton Steinberg

***

45

PRIVATE MEDITATIONS FOR HEALING

***

I give thanks to You, living and everlasting Spirit,
You have restored my soul within me.
Your faithfulness is abounding.

***

Heal me, Adonai, and I shall be healed.
Save me, and I shall be saved.
You are my Glory.

Jeremiah 17:14
***

Heal me, Adonai, for my bones shake with fear.
My whole being is fraught with anxiety.
How long, Adonai, how long?
Come back to me, Adonai, and rescue me.
Make me whole as I trust You will.

Psalm 6:3-5
***

Heal me, Adonai, as You say through Your prophet Jeremiah (30:17):
"For I will restore your health, and I will cure your wounds, says
Adonai."
***

I see your journey, and I bring healing. I will guide you and bring solace
to you,
and to those who support you I say:
It shall be well, well with those distant from Me,
and well with those near Me.
Says Adonai: I will heal you!

Isaiah 57:18-19
***

My God, the soul You give me is pure.
You create it, You form it, You breathe it into me,
And you watch over it inside me.

Siddur, Shaharit Prayer
***

FOR EVERYTHING A SEASON

(after Ecclesiastes 3:1-8)

For everything there is a season,
and a time for every experience under Heaven.

A time to be born and a time to die;
A time to grow and a time to shrink.

A time to lay seeds,
and a time to taste their fruit.

A time to hurt, and a time be well.

A time to give comfort, and a time to grieve.

A time to share, and a time to receive.

A time to love, and a time to be loved.

A time to study, and a time to germinate.

A time to work, and a time to rest.

A time to sail, and a time to drift.

A time to pause, and a time to rush forward.

A time to pray,
and a time to hold back from praying.

A time to ask forgiveness,
and a time to forgive others.

A time to be angry,
and a time to let go of anger.

A time to defend,
and a time for the peace of the brave.

Rabbi Dov Peretz Elkins

PRAYER

Just give me this:
A rinsing out, a cleansing free
Of all my smaller strivings
So I can be the class act God intended,
True to my purpose,
All my energy aligned behind my deepest intention.

And just this:
A quieting down,
A clearing away of internal ruckus,
So I can hear the huge stillness in my heart
And feel
How I pulse with all creation,
Part and parcel of Your great singing ocean.

And this too:
A willingness to notice and forgive the myriad times
I fall short,
Forgetting who I am,
What I really belong to.

So I can start over,
Fresh and clean,
Like sweet sheets billowing in the summer sun,
My heart pierced with gratitude.

Belleruth Naparstek

***

May I reach
That purest heaven, be to other souls
The cup of strength in some great agony,
Enkindle generous ardour, feed pure love,
Be the sweet presence of a good diffused,
And in diffusion ever more intense!
So shall I join the choir invisible
Whose music is the gladness of the world.

George Eliot
(Mary Ann Evans, d. 1880)

***

GOD, YOU ARE OUR FRIEND

I have no other helper than you, no other father,
I pray to you.
Only you can help me. My present misery is too great.
Despair grips me, and I am at my wit's end.
O Lord, Creator, Ruler of the World, Father,
I thank you that you have brought me through.

How strong the pain was--but you were stronger.
How deep the fall was--but you were even deeper.
How dark the night was--but you were the noonday
sun in it.
You are our father, our mother, our brother, and our
friend.

African prayer

***

Lead me to places of loneliness and pain.
May Your words shine in my mouth.
May I trust that the way You have made me
is the way that is needed.

Rachel Naomi Remen, M.D.

***

49

HOLINESS

HOLINESS EMCOMPASSES YOU

When there is no hatred, jealousy or competition,
a Light of Peace and a mighty audacity,
spring forth inside you.
The splendor of mercy, and the brilliance of Love
radiate through you.
The will to work and accomplish,
the fire to create and be restored,
The craving for quiet and for
the inner shout of jubilance -
These all join inside your Spirit–
And holiness encompasses you.

Rabbi Avraham Yitzhak Kook, *Orot HaKodesh*

***

THE YEARNING TO BE HOLY

May we find each other in the silence between the words.
May we heal the loneliness of our expertise with
the wisdom of our service.
May we honor in ourselves and all others
the deep and simple impulse to live,
To find sacred space and open land.
May we remember that the yearning to be holy
is a part of everyone
and the only hope for the next thousand years.

Rachel Naomi Remen, M.D.
Co-founder, Commonweal Cancer Help Program, California

***

INTEGRITY

The way to honesty in business is through the emulation of Adonai,
and through the imitation of God's attributes which are exalted and
upright.

For the way of Adonai is uprightness
And all God's deeds are faithfulness.

When one is honest and faithful, one thus walks in the steps of the
Creator.
God's seal is truth and if we want to serve God,
let our work bear the seal of truth.

When one sets out for business, let her recite this prayer:
"I am about to set forth to conduct my business, in faithfulness and
integrity,

So that my labor may help to reconcile God and the world.
Adonai, God of truth, grant me blessings in my efforts,
success in these endeavors,

and fulfill in me the words of your Scripture,
'Cast your burden upon Adonai, and Adonai will sustain you.' "

Adapted from *Shnay Luhot HaBrit (Two Tablets of the Covenant)* -
Rabbi Isaiah Horowitz (1570-1630)

***

The day returns and brings us the petty round of irritating concerns and
duties.

Help us to play the man, help us to perform them with laughter and kind
faces.

Let cheerfulness abound with industry.

Give us to go blithely on our business all this day,
bring us to our resting beds weary and content and undishonoured,

and grant us in the end the gift of sleep.

Robert Louis Stevenson 1850 - 1894

I NEED YOUR STRENGTH AND WISDOM

Great Spirit,
Whose voice I hear in the winds,
and whose breath gives life to all the world,
hear me! I am small and weak,
I need your strength and wisdom.

Let me walk in beauty,
and make my eyes ever behold the red and purple sunset.

Make my hands respect the things you have made
and my ears sharp to hear your voice.

Make me wise so that I may understand
the things that You have taught my people.

Let me learn the lessons
You have hidden in every leaf and rock.

I seek strength, not to be greater than the other,
but to fight my greatest enemy–myself.

Make me always ready to come to You
with clean hands and straight eyes.

So when life fades, as the fading sunset,
my spirit may come to You without shame.

Traditional Native American Prayer

***

GOD'S QUESTIONS

1. God won't ask what kind of car you drove, but will ask how many people you drove who didn't have transportation

2. God won't ask the square footage of your house, but will ask how many people you welcomed into your home

3. God won't ask about the fancy clothes you had in your closet, but will ask how many of those clothes helped the needy

4. God won't ask about your social status, but will ask what kind of class you displayed

5. God won't ask how many material possessions you had, but will ask if they dictated your life

6. God won't ask what your highest salary was, but will ask if you compromised your character to obtain that salary

7. God won't ask how much overtime you worked, but will ask if you worked overtime for your family and loved ones

8. God won't ask how many promotions you received, but will ask how you promoted others

9. God won't ask what your job title was, but will ask if you performed your job to the best of your ability

10. God won't ask what you did to help yourself, but will ask what you did to help others

11. God won't ask how many friends you had, but will ask how many people to whom you were a true friend

12. God won't ask what you did to protect your rights, but will ask what you did to protect the rights of others

13. God won't ask in what neighborhood you lived, but will ask how you treated your neighbors

14. God won't ask about the color of your skin, but will ask about the content of your character

15. God won't ask how many times your deeds matched your words, but will ask how many times they didn't

JERUSALEM

O JERUSALEM

Standing near the wall
Touching the ancient stone
Crowded all as one
I am not alone.

Traveling the patch
Footsteps on the shore.
Moving in the past
Where we have been before.

> *O Jerusalem, deep inside my heart*
> *O Jerusalem, never apart.*

Walking on and on
Many years ago
To a Promised Land
We have never known.

This will be our home
God has said to thee:
"A promise for all time
'Til eternity."

> *O Jerusalem, deep inside my heart*
> *O Jerusalem, never apart.*

Take my hand, O God.
Let me see the way.
Standing high above
Golden sunlit rays.

Full of strength and might
O Jerusalem,
City of Hope, City of Light,
My Jerusalem.

> *O Jerusalem, deep inside my heart*
> *O Jerusalem, never apart.*

Cantor Michell Kowitz

***

JERUSALEM OF THE TALMUD

There are ten portions of beauty in the world.
Nine are in Jerusalem, one in the rest of the world.

There are ten portions of suffering in the world.
Nine in Jerusalem, one in the rest of the world.

There are ten portions of wisdom in the world.
Nine in Jerusalem, one in the rest of the world.

There are ten portions of godlessness in the world.
Nine in Jerusalem, one in the rest of the world.

There are ten portions of Torah in the world.
Nine in Jerusalem, one in the rest of the world.

Avot de Rabbi Natan B 48

***

If one prays in Jerusalem it is as if one were praying before the Throne of
Glory,
for the very gate of heaven is located there, as it is written,
"This is the gateway to Heaven" (Genesis 28:17).

Midrash Tehillim 91:7

***

Jerusalem will be redeemed only through justice, as it is written,
"Zion will be redeemed through justice, and those who repent
through righteousness" Isaiah 1:27.

Talmud, Tractate Shabbat 139a

***

When one coats a wall of the house with plaster, one should leave a
small space
unfinished, in remembrance of Jerusalem.
When a woman adorns herself with jewels, she should leave something
off,
in remembrance of Jerusalem, as it is written,
"If I forget you, Yerushalayim, let my right hand wither" (Psalm 137:5).

Midrash Tehillim 137:6

***

55

CENTER OF THE WORLD

Eretz Yisrael is the Center of the world. Yerushalayim is the Center of Eretz Yisrael. The Bet HaMikdash (Temple) is the Center of Yerushalayim. The Heikhal (Hall) is the Center of the Bet HaMikdash. The Aron Kodesh (Holy Ark) is the Center of the Heikhal. The rock of the foundation is in front of the Aron Kodesh, and upon it the entire world is founded.

Midrash, Tahhuma, Kedoshim 10

***

HEARTS POUND - THE EXCITEMENT IS TREMENDOUS

The command came to move. The commander's half-track zoomed towards the Lions' Gate. Right behind, the rest of the troops sped ahead through the blackened arch of the Lions' Gate....

We arrive at the Mosque of Omar (the golden Dome of the Rock). From here to the Western Wall, it's only an extremely short distance. Men press forward quickly over the paving stones, as though pushed by a storm wind. Hearts pound; the excitement is tremendous. We are among the first to arrive at a small gate. From here, narrow, winding stairs lead us to the Western Wall. The Western Wall! Last remnant of the Temple. No Jew has set foot here for nineteen years. We are pushed ahead by the rising tide of soldiers...hundreds of dusty, perspiring paratroopers, their clothing stained with blood, crowd into the narrow rectangle in front of the Wall.... Hardened men, who for two solid days have waged war in pitched and bloody battles heavy with casualties, crying out loud with no shame - crying in excitement and release, in exaltation and recognition of the greatness and eternity of the Jewish people.

Yosef Argaman, *Ba-Mahaneh*, Israel Defense Forces

***

PINNACLE OF BEAUTY AND SPIRIT

As I travel around this land, which I saw for years in my dreams and prayers, its striking beauty and magnetic power are somehow more compelling than I expected. I find it impossible to comprehend how the variety of the entire world could be compressed into this tiny wedge of earth, with its hills and forests, its plains and deserts, its roaring waterfalls in the north down to the motionless surface of the Dead Sea. And in the center of all this stands Jerusalem, the pinnacle of beauty and spirit, the city of King David, which has united our people through these thousands of years.

Natan Sharansky, *Fear No Evil* (Random House, 1988)

***

KOL NIDRE

SACRED TIME

How much time did we waste
In the year that is now gone?

Did we fill our days with life
Or were they dull and empty?

Was there love inside our home
Or was the affectionate word left unsaid?

Was there a real companionship with our children
Or was there a living together and a growing apart?

Were we a help to our mates
Or did we take them for granted?

How was it with our friends:
Were we there when they needed us or not?

The mitzvah: did we perform it or postpone it?
The unnecessary gibe: did we say it or hold it back?

Were we sensitive to the rights and feelings of those who worked for us?

Did we acquire only possessions
Or did we acquire new insights as well?

Did we fear what the crowd would say
And keep quiet when we should have spoken out?

Did we mind only our own business
Or did we feel the heartbreak of others?

Did we live right, and if not,
Then can we learn; can we change?
can we turn to new directions?
Can we make "Teshuvah?"

Rabbi Allen S. Maller, *Tikkun Hanefesh*
Temple Akiba, Culver City, CA
***

LE-HAYIM - TO LIFE

LESSONS TO LIVE BY

We must alter our lives in order to alter our hearts,
for it is impossible to live one way and to pray another.

No one can be wrong with people and right with God.

What nobler ambition can a person have
than to cooperate with his or her Maker
in bringing about a better world in which to live?

*The great victories of life are most often won
in a quiet way,
and not with alarms and trumpets.*

The highest reward for a person's toil
is not what one gets for it
but what one becomes by it.

*Wisdom is not to be obtained from textbooks,
but must be coined out of human experience
in the flame of life.*

The universe is too great a mystery
for there to be only one single approach to it.

*God appeared in a bush
to teach us that the loftiest may be found in the lowliest.*

Every person born into this world represents something new,
something that never existed before,
something original and unique.

*Therefore, a person should so live that at the close of
every day
he or she can repeat: "I have not wasted my day."*

Compiled by Rabbi Bernard S. Raskas

***

N'EILAH

FOR A BETTER TOMORROW

You have taught us, O Lord,
that repentance does not merely mean
to feel sorry for yesterday.
The main purpose of repentance is to resolve to do better tomorrow.

*I pray to You, Lord,
at this hour of N'eilah twilight,
to help me measure everything I do
by the threefold yardstick of the ages:*

Will this deed of mine make me feel right inside?
Will it make me feel good and spiritually enriched?

*Will this deed of mine sanctify the name of God?
Will it sanctify the image of humanity in me?
Will it sanctify the name of the Jew?*

Will this deed of mine contribute to the Survival of Jews
and of Judaism in this land
for the next generation and for many generations to come?

*I pray to You, Lord,
make my repentance complete and sincere.*

May my thoughts, my feelings and my acts
be consecrated every day,
till next Yom Kippur and beyond
to Righteousness, Sanctification and Survival.

Rabbi Noah Golinkin

***

OPEN YOUR DOORS

Open your doors to us, Lord. The day goes down; the sun falls,
the sun disappears. Eternal, we come to your doors. We implore you:
Pardon us. We implore You: Have mercy upon us. Save us!

Nikos Kazantzakis

OPENING PRAYER

On the anniversary of Creation, Lord my God, comes a glimpse of the mystery of silence; out of the confines of chaos came the climax of cosmos. Your will subdued the matrix of stillness. You brought into being what had no form of independent existence; creativeness attained supremacy, out of which arose the order of the universe. Your power pervades all things in time and eternity.

On the threshold of Rosh Hashanah, I have entered the sacred precincts of Your house of worship. As the old year is vanishing, and the New Year is rising above the horizon, I am more aware of my deeper needs - truly the more profound longings of my being.

I lift my heart to You, O Heavenly Creator, in the quietness of the twilight hour of the New Year. Little do I know what is before me in the three hundred and threescore days ahead. Yet I fear not the untried morrow, for I put my total trust in You, upon whom I depend for guidance and guardianship.

On Rosh Hashanah, God of life, I pray to You for life abundant. Make my life imperative on moral rectitude, in conformity with the divine plan and purpose. Grant me a year of life filled with hope, health, and happiness.

I am now in readiness for divine worship. I draw nigh to You, my heavenly Guardian; in homage, I commune with You in spirit and in truth. Amen!

Rabbi Leo Ginsburg

***

WHERE ARE YOU?

God, where *are* You?

Where do I find you? You do not live here. You have no address.
The Universe is filled with Your glory. You live in every mountain,
and in every valley, and on the busy Pike outside.

You live in the beautiful riot of many colors of the Indian summer;
and you live in my soul.

And yet –I have built for You a special building,
beautiful, dignified, majestic, intimate, warm and friendly.

For whom did I build it?
For You and me. For our conversations together.
For Your glory, God, and for My humble need.

I should be talking to You--
when I see You in the beautiful sunrise,
when I see You in the innocent smile of a child,
when I see You in kind deeds.

But I forget. So I built this building.
I come here and remember to talk to You.

With the Psalmist I say:
Through Your abundant kindness I come into Your house,
and reverently I worship You, in Your holy sanctuary.

I love the habitation of Your house,
the place where Your glory dwells.

Rabbi Noah Golinkin

***

PEACE

(Adapted from excerpts of Prime Minister Yitzhak Rabin's final speech, to a pro-peace and anti-violence rally in Tel Aviv, November 4, 1995, the night he was assassinated):

I have always believed most of the nation wants peace and is prepared to take risks for peace. And you here, who have come to take a stand for peace, as well as many others who are not here, are proof that the nation truly wants peace and rejects violence. Violence is undermining the foundations of Israeli democracy. It must be rejected and condemned and it must be contained. It is not the way of the State of Israel. Democracy is our way....

I was a soldier for 27 years. I fought as long as there was no prospect of peace. I believe that there is now a chance for peace, a great chance, which must be seized....

Peace is not just a prayer. It is at first a prayer, but it is also the realistic aspiration of the Jewish people. But peace has its enemies, who are trying to harm us, to torpedo the peace.

We have found a partner in peace among the Palestinians as well - the PLO, which was an enemy and has now forsaken terrorism.... There is no painless way forward for Israel. But the way of peace is preferable to war....

This rally must send a message to the Israeli public, to the Jews of the world, to the multitudes in the Arab lands, and in the world at large, that the nation of Israel wants peace, supports peace—and for this, I thank you.

***

May Adonai support us all the day long,
till the shadows lengthen,

and the evening comes,
and the busy world is hushed,

And the fever of life over,
and our work is done.

Then in God's mercy, may Adonai give us a safe lodging,
and a holy rest, and peace at the last.

Adapted from John Henry Newman 1801 - 1890

***

A CALL TO THE WORLD

We, the peoples of this earth, bear the ultimate responsibility for what happens to our world.

We hold life to be infinitely precious. It must be cherished, nurtured, respected.

If these beliefs are to have reality, we must accept duties to each other and to the generations to come.

We have the duty to ennoble life on earth and to protect it against assault, indignity, injustice, discrimination, hunger, disease and abuse.

We have the duty to safeguard the conditions of existence, to develop and use the world's resources for the human good, to protect and preserve the soil so that it will yield ample food, to keep air and water free of poisons.

Above all, we have the duty to save our world and everything in it from the consequences of senseless violence in a nuclear age.

We have the duty to create the conditions of durable peace on earth, so that people neither have to kill nor to be killed.

We have the duty to use our intelligence and knowledge in the making of a bountiful life on earth for human beings and to encourage the full development of each individual.

In order to carry out these duties, we must assert the primary allegiance of every man, woman and child to the whole human race.

As citizens of the human race, we have the right to demand an end of anarchy in the dealings among nations. World anarchy produces untold horror and anguish and can lead only to the disintegration of society and to the destruction of life itself.

We have the right to demand that nations submit to law among themselves, just as they require that citizens submit to law inside nations.

We have the right to demand that nations adhere to world law, replacing the irrational, irresponsible, and violent behavior of nations with orderly and workable methods for insuring a creative and just peace.

In making known these duties and rights, and in asserting a higher allegiance, we pledge ourselves to the goal of a world made safe and fit for human beings, animals and vegetation.

Anonymous

***

"MAY THE ONE WHO MADE PEACE...."

A prominent Jewish prayer concludes "May the One who made peace in the heavens grant peace to us on earth." What does it mean to create peace in the heavens? Ancient man looked up into the sky and he saw the sun and the rainclouds. And he would say to himself "How can fire and water, sun and rain co-exist in the same sky? Either the water would put out the fire, or the fire would dry up the water." How do they get along? It must be a miracle. The sun says, "If I dry up the rainclouds, as I probably could, the world will not survive without rain." The clouds say, "If we extinguish the sun, the world will perish in darkness." So the fire and the water make peace, realizing that if either one of them achieved a total victory, the world could not endure.

When we pray for God to grant us the sort of peace ordained in the heavens, this is the miracle we ask for. How can men and women live together happily? They are opposites; their needs are different, their rhythms are different. It takes a miracle for them to bridge those differences and unite the masculine side of God's image with the feminine side.

How can Arabs and Israelis learn to live together? Irish Catholics and Irish Protestants? Black South Africans and white South Africans? It takes a miracle for them to realize that if they won, if they had it all and the other side had nothing, the world could not survive their victory. Only by making room for everyone in the world, even for our enemies, can the world survive.

May God who showed us the miracle of Shalom, of making room for each other and giving up the illusion of victory in the heavens, grant a similar miracle to all of us who inhabit the earth.

Rabbi Harold S. Kushner

***

PRAISE TO YOU, GOD

Let us imagine a world without color, without regal red or leafy green, a world that bores the eye with gray.

> *Praise to You, God, for all the colors in the rainbow,*
> *for eyes that are made for seeing and for beauty*
> *that is its own excuse for being.*

Let us imagine a world without sound, a world where deathly silence covers the earth like a shroud.

> *Praise to You, God, for words that speak to our minds,*
> *for songs that lift our spirits, and for all those souls*
> *who know how to listen.*

Let us imagine a world without order, where no one can predict the length of the day or the flow of the tide. Imagine a universe where planets leave their orbits and soar like meteors through the heavens and where the law of gravity is repealed at random.

> *Praise to You, God, for the marvelous order of nature,*
> *from stars in the sky to particles in the atom.*

Let us imagine a world without love, a world in which the human spirit , incapable of caring, is locked in the prison of the self.

> *Praise to You, God, for the capacity to feel happiness in*
> *another's happiness and pain in another's pain.*

As the universe whispers of a Oneness behind all that is, so the love in the human heart calls on people everywhere to unite in pursuit of those ideals that make us human.

> *As we sing of One God, we rejoice in the wonder of*
> *the universe and we pray for that day when all humanity will*
> *be one.*

Rabbi Henry Cohen

***

PRAYER

Public worship draws out the latent life in the human spirit.
Those who, when alone, do not, or cannot, pray, find an impulse to prayer
when they worship with others;

*And some will pray together who cannot pray alone, as many
will sing in chorus who would not sing solos.*

Many who are spiritually weak in themselves find spiritual strength
in a common spiritual effort.

That is the value of public worship for the individual....

A congregation at worship is a society declaring its devotion to God,
a community forged by faith in God.

*Here is an experience that can deepen the social spirit
and strengthen the bond of sympathy among men and women.*

If in public worship I realise that my prayers
are also the prayers of the person by my side,
it will make us more effectively aware of our common humanity....

*Those who worship together bring God into their mutual relations.
If public worship does not produce this result,
then it is but private worship in a public place.*

If it does bring men and women close together under the influence of
God,
then it is a way to the sanctification of human society.

Siddur Lev Chadash

***

He prayeth best, who loveth best
All things both great and small;
For the dear God who loveth us,
He made and loveth all.

Samuel Taylor Coleridge

***

66

A PRAYER FOR PRAYER

My God
My soul's companion
My heart's precious friend
I turn to You.

I need to close out the noise
To rise above the noise
The noise that interrupts-
The noise that separates-
The noise that isolates.
I need to hear You again.

In the silence of my innermost being,
In the fragments of my yearned-for wholeness,
I hear whispers of Your presence-
Echoes of the past when You were with me
When I felt Your nearness
When together we walked-
When You held me close, embraced me in Your love,
laughed with me in my joy.
I yearn to hear You again.
In your oneness, I find healing.
In the promise of Your love, I am soothed.
In Your wholeness, I too can become whole again.

Please listen to my call-
help me find the words
help me find the strength within
help me shape my mouth, my voice, my heart
so that I can direct my spirit and find You in prayer
In words only my heart can speak
In songs only my soul can sing
Lifting my eyes and heart to You.

Adonai S'fatai Tiftach–open my lips, precious God,
so that I can speak with You again.

Rabbi Sheldon Zimmerman

***

67

GOD, OUR FRIEND

Almighty God, we thank You for this hour of prayer,
this precious opportunity of realizing Your presence,

Of laying before You our desires, our hopes, our gratitude.
Of all blessed things the realization of Your presence is the most blessed.

How empty would our life be without it.
Without You, in the maze of our confused world, if we did not come back

From time to time to commune with You,
to receive the assurance of Your existence and Your love.

How good it is to know that You are with us,
in all our difficulties and times of distress,

To feel that in You we have one Friend
Whose help is sure, whose love is unchangeable.

Anonymous

***

WHAT IS PRAYER?

It is the wind passing through the trees, and the sun glittering in the
water.
It is the snow melting its way down the mountain, and the rain drumming
on the roof.

It is a child bringing you a flower of summer, and the song of a bird high
in the clouds.
It is the first step of a new-born, or the tears of his first hurt.

It is the old one sitting in the sun, or the song of the harvest in the fields.
It is the laughter of happiness, or the weeping of desolation.

It is the outstretched hand of your mother and father, and the shared
dreams and hopes.
It is the beauty of creation and the awareness of the Creator.

It is the hope and despair, dreams and acceptance, smiles and tears –
song and music.
What is prayer? All of your creation, God!

High Holy Day Family Service, Stephen S. Wise Temple, Los Angeles

It is prayer that restores to us the ability to feel,
to see, and to appreciate.

Rabbi Reuven Hammer

***

Night is drawing nigh.
For all that has been–Thanks!
For all that shall be–Yes!

Dag Hammarskjold

***

THE POWER OF GOD

May the power of God this day enable me,
the nakedness of God disarm me,
the beauty of God silence me,
the justice of God give me voice,
the integrity of God hold me,
the desire of God move me,
the fear of God expose me to the truth,
the breath of God give me abundant life.

Janet Morley

***

Lord, behold our family here assembled.
We thank you for this place in which we dwell,
for the love which unites us,
for the peace accorded us this day,
for the hope with which we expect the morrow;
for the health, the work, the food and the bright skies,
that make our lives delightful;
for our friends all parts of the earth. Amen.

Robert Louis Stevenson

***

Grant me to recognize in others, Lord God,
the radiance of Your own face.

Teilhard de Chardin

***

GOD, HELP ME TO PRAY

God, early in the morning I cry to You. Help me to pray
And to concentrate my thoughts on You: I cannot do this alone.

*In me there is darkness, but with You there is light;
I am lonely, but You do not leave me;*

I am feeble in heart, but with You there is help;
I am restless, but with You there is peace.

*In me there is bitterness, but with You there is patience;
I do not understand Your ways, but You know the way for me...*

Restore me to liberty, and enable me so to live now
That I may answer before You and before me.

Lord, whatever this day may bring, Your name be praised.

Dietrich Bonhoeffer

***

REDEMPTION

DISCOVERY

No one ever told me the coming of the Messiah
Could be an inward thing.

No one ever told me a change of heart
Might be as quiet as new-fallen snow.

No one ever told me that redemption
Was as simple as springtime and as wonderful

As birds returning after a long winter,
Rose-breasted grosbeaks singing in the swaying branches
Of a newly budded tree.

No one every told me that salvation
Might be like a fresh spring wind
Blowing away the dried, withered leaves of another year,
Carrying the scent of flowers, the promise of fruition.

What I found for myself I try to tell you:
Redemption and salvation are very near,
And the taste of them is in the world
That God created and laid before us.

Ruth F. Brin

Harvest: Collected Poems and Prayers
Reconstructionist Press, 1986
Reprinted by permission of Ruth F. Brin

***

Be a disciple of Aaron: loving peace and pursuing peace, loving your fellow creatures and attracting them to the study of Torah.

A COMMITMENT TO JEWISH VALUES

We accept our Jewishness and we will strive to live as intelligent and educated Jews aware of our past and prepared for our future.

We declare our loyalty to world Jewry and will answer our responsibilities to see all Jews as part of one entity.

We re-pledge our loyalty to *Eretz Yisrael* and will make every effort to help our brothers and sisters who reside in our Holy Land.

We will maintain our full identity with the American Jewish community rejoicing in the fact of democracy in Jewish life.

We rededicate ourselves to the principles of social justice for all peoples. We accept the command of Judaism to work for the rights and freedoms of every child of God.

We affirm the unity of the human race and we will strive to conduct ourselves with dignity and with love toward all.

We rededicate ourselves to our families. We shall strive to understand our families and to give them every ounce of our love and loyalty.

We solemnly pledge that we will strive to the best of our abilities to live with high personal standards and to constantly seek moral perfection.

Help us, God, to maintain these values. When we falter, be with us. May Your understanding and strength abide with us this day and throughout the rest of the year.

May God give us strength and bless us with peace.

Rabbi Bernard Raskas

***

I HAVE A DREAM

This is our hope,
this is the faith that I go back South with.

*With this faith we will be able to hew
out of the mountain of despair a stone of hope.*

With this faith we will be able to transform
the jangling discords of our nation
into a beautiful symphony of brotherhood.

*With this faith we will be able to work together,
to pray together, to struggle together,
to go to jail together,*

To stand up for freedom together,
knowing that we will be free one day....

Martin Luther King, Jr.
Lincoln Memorial - August 28, 1963

***

73

A PRAYER TO THE SHEKHINAH

Come be our mother   we are your young ones
Come be our bride   we are your lover
Come be our dwelling   we are your inhabitants
Come be our game   we are your players
Come be our punishment   we are your sinners
Come be our ocean   we are your swimmers
Come be our victory   we are your army
Come be our laughter   we are your story
Come be our Shekhinah   we are your glory
We believe that you live
Though you delay   we believe you will certainly come.

When the transformation happens as it must
When we remember
When she wakes from her long repose in us
When she wipes the nightmare
Of history from her eyes
When she returns from exile
When she utters her voice in the streets
In the opening of the gates
When she enters the modern world
When she crosses the land
Shaking her breasts and hips
With timbrels and with dances
Magnified and sanctified
Exalted and honored
Blessed and glorified
When she causes tyranny to vanish
When she and he meet
When they behold each other face to face
When they become naked and not ashamed
On that day will our God be One
And their name One.

Shekhinah bless us and keep us
Shekhinah shine your face on us
Shekhinah turn your countenance
To us and give us peace.

Alicia Ostriker
The Nakedness of Our Fathers (Rutgers University Press, 1994)

***

74

RENEWAL

A NEW YEAR

We enter a new year, each year
As if we were entering a new home

We pass over a threshold in time,
Through new doors, to a new life

The year that is past casts a shadow,
A shadow of nostalgia and memory

Yet as spirits soar, and optimism
Lights the new rooms of life

The twelve-month house of life
To come seems bright and cheery

We pray for portals of peace,
We ask for windows of serenity

We petition for beams of security
We hope for light and health

May our prayers be answered,
May our New Home, our New Year be
Strong, alive and full of love.

Rabbi Sylvan D. Kamens

***

Ha-yashan yit-hadesh v'he-hadash yit-kadesh

The old will be renewed, and the new will be sanctified.

Rabbi Avraham Yitzhak Kook
Iggrot Ha-Rayah, Volume 1, letter 214, line 30
(Jerusalem: Mosad HaRav Kook)

***

75

SCRIPTURAL READINGS

RECONCILIATION

[Can be read before Torah lesson of first day of Rosh Hashanah]

The threat to our salvation is the clash of peoples:
Jews and Arabs
offspring of a single father,
separated in youth by jealousy,
in adolescence by fear,
in adulthood by power,
in old age by habit.
It is time to break these habits of hate
and create new habits:
habits of the heart
that will awake within us
the causeless love of redemption and peace.

Rabbi Rami M. Shapiro

***

YOM KIPPUR

We don't have to stare in wonder at the moon.
We can go there.

We don't have to exorcise devils anymore.
We have drugs to change our personalities.

We don't have to read old books
When new ideas sweep the earth.

Why, then, do we have to do today
What our ancestors did?

Or have we not changed?
Are we still primitive people
Doing again and again
Things we know are evil?

Must we always fight against ourselves?
Is that battle never won?

"And you shall afflict yourselves.
It is a law forever."

If we cannot win the battle,
Help us, at least, not to lose it.
It is better to struggle forever
Then to die once.

Leviticus 16:31

Rabbi Michael Hecht

***

The
average
person
is not
average

SELF-ESTEEM

I AM THE REFLECTION OF YOU

Help me to let go of my preoccupations
with the future.
Give me the strength to stop
my futile attempts
to predict and control the future.

*Let me see no value in my plan
of what the future should be.*

Rid me of my senseless questions
about tomorrow
And of all my desires to manipulate
and control others.

*Remind me that my fears and uncertainties
of tomorrow are only related to
my unfounded fear of You.*

Help me be still
help me listen and love.

*Awaken me to the truth of Your Presence
being only in the now of this moment.
Lift me up into Your Arms
and remind me that I am your Creation,
and that I am the Perfection of Love.*

Help me to acknowledge that I am your Messenger
of Love, and free me to shine Your Light everywhere.

*Let me feel Your freedom within me, and
let me laugh at the illusions
that my ego once made me feel were so real.*

Let me be the Light; let me be joy;
Let me know that I am
the reflection of You wherever I am
and wherever I go.

Gerald G. Jampolsky

***

79

SERVICE (AVODAH)

CONTEMPORARY INTERPOLATIONS FOR THE AVODAH SERVICE

Interpolation for the Introduction, describing preparation of Kohen Gadol

Ten days before Yom Kippur, we gathered in the synagogue on Rosh Hashanah to begin our period of preparation for the Day of Atonement. We read prayers, listened to the chant of the Service, studied Torah, listened to the words of sermons that encouraged us to examine our ways. Hopefully we have used these days to search our heart, so on this day we know enough of ourselves to make confession before the awesomeness of the Holy One. We have dressed this day in clothing appropriate to the specialness of the day, cleansed ourselves so that we may purge from ourselves those unwanted aspects of our lives that sully us, and hinder us from the completeness of life.

Interpolation for First Confession: Anee U'Veitee

Many times during the course of the year have I awakened in the night, having tossed and turned, restless from a gnawing sensation, tense and discomforted from the weight imposed upon me from a sense of foreboding. From the clarity that emerges from wrestling with a problem, that undergirded many of my actions, I realized that I was misleading myself, and resolved to rectify my ways. I resolved, as I did last Yom Kippur, to change my priorities. All too often, after resolving in my mind to change, now calmed I fell back to sleep, wakening refreshed, not, in actuality, to change my ways.

At times during the past year, I, and my household, have behaved in ways that have not brought honor upon ourselves. At times, I have hid behind my family, claiming that a questionable act I was doing was to benefit them; when in reality the only one to benefit was myself. Members of my family have also hid behind me, claiming that questionable act was for my benefit, when in reality it was only for theirs. Singly and together we have not always been true to our word.

We spend this day in contemplative prayer, so that we may understand and then confess our wrongdoings, and those of our household. In the words of the Kohen Gadol, "God, I have committed iniquity, I have transgressed, I have sinned against you, I and my household. I beseech you...."

***

80

Interpolation for Second Confession: "V'ha-Kohaneem"

The Torah enjoined the Kohanim, the priests, with the responsibility of leading the people, and looking after their well-being. Many of us assume positions of responsibility with the community, as did the Kohanim, the priests of Biblical days. We are members of Boards of Directors, professionals with standing in organizations and institutions, physicians, teachers, social workers, accountants, lawyers, and members of other professions that advise and lead people and work for their well-being. During the course of the year we have, at times, become confused. We have, at times, purposely, or inadvertently, misled, misdirected. We have posed as working for altruistic purposes, and at times have won the acclaim of members of the community for the donation of our time, our resources, and our energy. And yet, when we alone sometimes delved into the motivations of our actions, we realize that we may not have acted out of a sense of altruism, but out of a deep selfishness, a deep need to feed our egos by placing ourselves in positions of power. Have we confused our own needs with those of the community? In our own decision making process have we rationalized our own quest for power, and through our cunning and hard work, imposed, upon others?

On this Yom Kippur, we need to scrutinize our actions on behalf of our communities. We can obfuscate the truth so that others will not discern it. We may even, for a period of time, hide from ourselves. But we cannot hide from You, the One who searches the motivations of our hearts, but Who judges us with compassionate truth.

Interpolation for Third Confession "K'hal Yisrael"

Not always does a community act responsibly. Hunger and starvation abound. People are oppressed, and little more than lip service is paid to the amelioration of the ills. People go hungry, die for lack of health care. And yet society ignores or rationalizes the death, the hunger, the malevolent forces that degrade some and permit others to trample them, and rise on their backs, often times with a gentle smile and a polite, "O excuse me." We are the pioneers. Each and every day the sun shines anew, and the moon casts its reflections, and in the newness of the day, we who venture forth as pioneers forging their way through the day quiescently, do little to overturn this betrayal. We, each of us, you and I, pioneers of the day, are also the oppressors of the day.

The High Priest, after the third confession went into the Holy of Holies, emerged after a time with the glorious words, "Va-yomer Adonai Salahtee K'd'varekha." God has said, "I have forgiven as you asked."

81

God, we try to search our hearts, as we attempt to discern our ways. We work to accomplish the difficult task of stripping our defenses from ourselves. We attempt to strip away all pretenses. Being honest with ourselves, and with You, is difficult; it is not always pleasant. Help us make our confessions before You, as You did the High Priest. May we always have the faith, that in love and compassion, our confessions, our deepest secrets, our hidden truths will be, to You and to us, a source of blessing. Bless us, God, that we may have the courage to ultimately come closer to You through honest confession.

Rabbi Daniel A. Jezer

***

The presence of LOVE makes us aware of why we are here

THE PRIVILEGE OF SERVING

Hineni, sh'lahaynee - Send me, God, as Your messenger,
To all hearts who lack a home,

Hineni, sh'lahaynee - Send me, God, as Your messenger,
To all those who live without love.

Hineni, sh'lahaynee - Send me, God, as your messenger,
To all flocks that have no shepherd.

Hineni, sh'lahaynee - Send me, God, as your messenger,
To all youth who have never been blessed.

Hineni, sh'lahaynee - Send me, God, as your messenger,
To the hungry who have not been fed.

Hineni, sh'lahaynee - Send me, God, as your messenger,
To those whose face is bowed in dust, with none to lift them up.

Hineni, sh'lahaynee - Send me, God, as your messenger,
To those in grief, whose tears have not been dried.

Hineni, sh'lahaynee - Send me, God, as your messenger,
To those imprisoned, whose bars have not been pried open.

Let me, Adonai, burn with love of Your Torah,
That others' hearts may be kindled with the performance of
Mitzvot.

May my humble soul, Adonai,
be illumined with Knowledge of You,
That others' paths may be lit up with clarity of purpose.

Permit my humble hands, God, be quick to do Your service.
May my simple being always stand ready
for my share of Tikkun Olam.

Let service to You and Your children
Always be my highest calling, now and always.

Rabbi Dov Peretz Elkins

***

WHOM CAN I LOVE AND SERVE?

We may wonder whom can I love and serve?
Where is the face of God to whom I can pray?
The answer is simple. That naked one. That lonely one.
That unwanted one is my brother and my sister.
If we have no peace, it is because we have forgotten
that we belong to each other.

Mother Teresa

***

YOU ARE A MESSENGER OF THE MOST HIGH

Each lifetime is the pieces of a jigsaw puzzle.
For some there are more pieces.
For others the puzzle is more difficult to assemble.
Some seem to be born with a nearly completed puzzle.

And so it goes.
Souls going this way and that
Trying to assemble the myriad parts.

But know this. You do not have within yourself
All the pieces to your puzzle.
Like before the days when they used to seal
Jigsaw puzzles in cellophane.
Insuring that all the pieces were there.

Everyone carries with them at least one and probably
Many pieces to someone else's puzzle.
Sometimes they know it.
Sometimes they don't.

And when you present your piece
Which is worthless to you,
To another, whether you know it or not,
Whether they know it or not,
You are a messenger from the Most High.

Rabbi Lawrence Kushner

***

SHABBAT

TO MAKE ME STOP... SEE... HEAR...

God, *when* shall I seek You?
I should seek You every hour, every day,

But I am busy. I run through life.
In my busy-ness are many sounds I do not hear.
As I run through this beautiful world
there are many sights I do not see.

I am glad You made a Sabbath day to make me stop;
to make me see, and make me hear
the Symphony of color, the Fantasia of sounds
of birds, and trees and rivers and skies.

I am glad You made me a Sabbath day, so I can sing
with David, the shepherd and the King.

Come let us sing unto the Lord.
Let us joyfully acclaim the Rock of our salvation.
Let the heavens be glad and the earth rejoice.
Let the sea roar and all within it give praise.

Let the field and all within it exalt,
Let all the trees of the forest sing before the Lord.

Rabbi Noah Golinkin

***

SHABBAT

Let us sing a song of Shabbat.

You are a day. You are a way.
You are a Way of Life.
Six days of the week we toil and run.
on the seventh day we cease.

Shabbat, you are a Day of Peace.

You are a family together, at home.
Talking, not shouting.
Listening, sharing, singing together.

You are a congregation together, in the Synagogue.
The warm glance; the friendly word.
Feeling part of one another. Praying together.

Shabbat, you are a Day of Equality.

The world is not divided into masters and slaves.
Everyone works six days a week.
Everyone stops - on the seventh day.

Shabbat, you are a Day of Rest.

Walking, not running. Walking leisurely to Shul.
All business has stopped. Commerce has stopped.
Time has stopped. A nap in the afternoon.

Shabbat, you are a Day of Beauty.

Everything shines today:
The tablecloth, the silverware, the Hallah cover, the bottle of wine,
the candles, the face of the one who kindles the lights;
the face of the child, who beholds all this beauty.

Shabbat, you are a Way of Holiness.

I sing a song to you.
I am going your way.

Rabbi Noah Golinkin

***
86

FIRST A SPARK

First a spark
then candle glow.

I watched you at sunset time
eyes sparkling in Shabbat light.

Circling above the flames,
my hands pulled
the warmth of Shabbat peace inside.

Praying for a good week and for blessing.

Take time - the lights beckon
for dreams and wonder,
for the candles grow smaller,
the children taller, even as we pray.

Hold this sunset moment and let it go
into morning light.

Another generation's candlesticks
receive the next generation's lights.

And somewhere in the middle
we stand, holding hands
with yesterday and tomorrow
linking echoes of ancient melodies
with the breath of our children.

Finding God and hope in their embrace,
renewing days of creation.

In ordinary time - remember -
First a spark
and then candle glow.

Rabbi Sandy Eisenberg Sasso

***
87

HA-SHOAH

For Holocaust Memorial Services and Yom Kippur Martyrology

***

WRINGING HAPPINESS OUT OF LIFE

"...I often asked myself why I didn't feel more vindictive. Maybe my religious faith played a role in the situation. Only God can take vengeance and punish, not a human being. Feelings of hatred are an expression of powerlessness, and I always concentrated on being as strong as possible, for myself and for others.

"I allowed my thoughts to delve to a deeper philosophical level only when there was some chance it would help me. Other than that, I tried my very best to stay out of the way of dangers and conflicts that threatened me. And I mustered strength from the individual moments of happiness that I was always able to wring out of life, no matter how dire the straits."

Gad Beck, *An Underground Life: The Memoirs of a Gay Jew in Nazi Berlin*
(Trans. Allison Brown, The University of Wisconsin Press, 1999)

***

THE KINGDOM OF NIGHT

Never shall I forget that night, the first night in camp, which has turned my life into one long night, seven times cursed and seven times sealed. Never shall I forget that smoke. Never shall I forget the little faces of children, whose bodies I saw turned to wreaths of smoke beneath a silent blue sky.

Never shall I forget those flames which consumed my faith forever.

Never shall I forget that nocturnal silence which deprived me, for all eternity, of the desire to live. Never shall I forget those moments which murdered my God and my soul and turned my dreams to dust. Never shall I forget these things, even if I am condemned to live as long as God Himself. Never.

Elie Wiesel, *Night* (Hill & Wang, 1969)

***

THE IMPORTANCE OF SPEAKING OUT

In connection with the plague of the frogs . . . a strange expression is used. The Torah says, "Va-yaal HATS'FARDEYA," that *one* frog came up. Then it says, "The *frogs* came up and covered the land of Egypt." Isn't that a strange expression? What was it -- one frog, or many, that inundated Egypt?

Listen to what the Talmudic Sages say. First, one frog came up. No one reacted, and so he gave the signal, and other frogs followed him and soon, they covered the whole land of Egypt.

What were the Rabbis saying when they created this Midrash? Were they really only talking about frogs? Were they really only responding to a peculiarity in the biblical text? Perhaps. But I have a hunch that they were talking about more than frogs. What they were saying is that when one destructive, dangerous force arises, those who would join him, those who would be like him, wait to see what will happen to him. If nobody minds, if he climbs up out of the mire and nobody chases him away, then the other frogs follow him, and soon they cover the land.

Perhaps that is what happens often in history. One television program, watched by millions, mocks and maligns the Jewish people and religion. And we say nothing. We take it, as if it were socially acceptable to insult us and our religion on national television. And the message goes forth that it is all right, that no one minds, that it is permissible to attack the Jews and Judaism. And soon, others see that and follow.

That is what I think the Sages of the Midrash meant when they said that one frog came out of the mud first, and when no one minded, when no one protested, it gave the signal, and soon, many more followed.

Rabbi Jack Riemer

***

WHAT CAN WE SAY?

Judaism and Christianity do not merely tell of God's love for humanity.
They stand or fall on their fundamental claim
that the human being is of ultimate and absolute value.
The Holocaust poses the most radical counter-testimony
to both Judaism and Christianity.
No statement, theological or otherwise,
should be made that would not be credible
in the presence of burning children.

Rabbi Irving (Yitz) Greenberg

AN OATH

In the presence of eyes
which witnessed the slaughter,
which saw the oppression
the heart could not bear,
and as witness the heart
that once taught compassion
until days came to pass
that crushed human feeling,
I have taken an oath: To remember it all,
to remember, not once to forget!
Forget not one thing to the last generation
when degradation shall cease,
to the last, to its ending,
when the rod of instruction
shall have come to conclusion.
An oath: Not in vain passed over
the night of terror.
An oath: No morning shall see
me at flesh pots again.
An oath: Lest from this we learned nothing.

Abraham Shlonsky

(The original poem may be seen in the Yad Vashem Holocaust Memorial
in Jerusalem.)

***

90

POLAND: THE MARCH OF THE LIVING
Just Like Me

Jody Krasner, age 16, Toronto, Ontario

Those victims of man's hatred
were children just like me.
Those who once had normal lives
were children just like me.
Those uprooted from their lives
Those dragged from their homes in the middle of the night
were children just like me.
Those robbed of everything they had
were children just like me.
Those locked behind a ghetto wall
were children just like me.
Those struck by pain and poverty
were children just like me.
Those taken by starvation and disease
were children just like me.
Those forced to brave the endless winters
were children just like me.
Those who never saw the outside world
were children just like me.
Those left orphaned in the streets
were children just like me.
Those robbed of their childhood
were children just like me.
Those robbed of their smiles
were children just like me.
Those who never even had a chance
were children just like me.
Those ripped from the arms of their mothers
were children just like me.
Those shipped in from far-off lands
were children just like me.
Those forced to stand for days on end
were children just like me.
Those killed before their time
were children just like me.
Those marched unwillingly to their deaths
were children just like me.

Those stripped and shot and gassed and burnt
were children just like me.
Those buried in pits, in unmarked graves
were children just like me.
Those all too young to die
were children just like me.

Those flickering lights in a cold dark world
were children just like me.
Those silent soldiers who fought off the darkness
were children just like me.
Those one and a half million innocent souls
were children just like me.
Yes, those children of the Holocaust
were children just like me.
And you, who killed my neighbors, my friends and my family, you too,
were children just like me.

Liturgies on the Holocaust: An Interfaith Anthology,
ed. Marcia Sachs Littell and Sharon Weissman Gutman

***

Not all victims were Jews, but all Jews were victims.   Elie Wiesel

LORD, GIVE US STRENGTH

Lord, as we gather today,
We pray for courage and for strength

When we remember the evils in the past,
The innocents tortured, maimed, and murdered,

We are almost afraid to make ourselves remember.
But we are even more afraid to forget.

We ask for wisdom, that we might mourn,
And not be consumed by hatred.
That we might remember, and yet not lose hope.

We must face evil –
And, so doing, reaffirm our faith in future good.

We cannot erase yesterday's pains,
but we can vow that they will not have been suffered in vain.

And so, we pray: For those who were given death,
Let us choose life—
for us and for generations yet to come.

For those who found courage to stand against evil—
often at the cost of their lives –
Let us vow to carry on their struggle.

We must teach ourselves, and our children:
To learn from hate that we must love,
To learn from evil to live for good.

**

Liturgies on the Holocaust: An Interfaith Anthology,
ed. Marcia Sachs Littell and Sharon Weissman Gutman

***

SHOFAR

THE SHOFAR CALLS

The shofar calls: T'kiah

Arise! Awake! Come from your beds, your homes
to the blast that calls you, the siren that warns you:
seek shelter for your spirit; enter now the opening gates.

The ram's horn cries: Sh'varim

Worship in truth, pray together in confidence and in trust,
determined that promises shall be kept, oaths fulfilled,
words spoken thoughtfully in honor and in truth.

The shrill notes tremble: T'ruah

Listen to the cries of the ancient martyrs,
Sense the unbearable silence of the dead,
Contemplate in reverence and awe
all those who died "Al Kiddush HaShem"
(for the sanctity of God's name)

The shofar blasts: T'kiah G'dolah

Remember! Recall the ages of our people,
Dwell on your own life in the year that has passed,
Call up from the darkness the mistakes, the errors,
the evil deeds that you must deal with now.

Three times three the great horn blows: T'kiah, Sh'varim, T'ruah

Return! Return to God Who made you,
Arise to prayer, awake to memory, achieve repentance,
Return to God Who loves you,
Now while the Days of Awe are passing,
before the closing of the gates.

Ruth Brin, from *The Hush of Midnight,*
Adas Israel Congregation, Washington, DC

***

94

SHOFAR SERVICE

The shofar is the preeminent Rosh Hashanah symbol. How can we be inspired by the sound of the Shofar to seek peace? The word *shalom* has so many meanings in our tradition. We say *"Shalom"* as we welcome another person into our presence.

> *May the shofar of* shalom *help us greet each person with a cheerful countenance.*

So, too, when we take leave of another human being we say the words *"Shalom,* may you go in peace."

> *May the shofar of* shalom *help us peacefully to leave one another's presence inspired by these Ten Days of Awe.*

Our Bible, Rabbinic literature and Siddurim are filled with teachings yearning for peace.

> *May the shofar of* shalom *call us -* "Sim Shalom Ba-Olam," *God help us bring peace into our world. May the shofar of* shalom *inspire us -* "Shalom Rav Al Yisrael Amkha," *to work to create true and lasting peace for all who dwell on earth.*

Shalom is also part of the world we use to describe how we value family harmony and domestic tranquillity - *Shalom Bayit.*

> *May the shofar of* shalom *call us to continue to strive for* shalom bayit *for those we love.*

We pray - *"Oseh Shalom Bimromav, Hu Ya-aseh Shalom Aleiniu,"* God Who makes peace in the heavens, grant peace to us and to all Your children.

> *May the shofar of* shalom *help us to create peace in God's world.*

The Talmud and Jewish Law Codes instruct us to seek peace in our relationships with all human beings at all times and all occasions.

> *Shalom is derived from the Hebrew root,* shalame, *wholeness, security and tranquillity. May the shofar of* shalom *help us realize that true* shalom *starts as we search for inner peace.*

Rabbis Jonathan Ginsburg and Julie K. Gordon
95

A GREAT SHOFAR IS SOUNDED,
A STILL SMALL VOICE IS HEARD

"You open the Book of Remembrance,
and it speaks for itself,
For each of us has signed it with deeds."
This is the sobering truth,
Which both frightens and consoles us:

Each of us is an author,
Writing, with deeds, in life's Great Book.
And to each You have given the power,
To write lines that will never be lost.

No song is so trivial,
No story is so commonplace,
No deed is so insignificant,
That You do not record it.

No kindness is ever done in vain;
Each act leaves its imprint;
All our deeds, the good and the bad,
Are noted and remembered by You.

So help us to remember always,
That what we do will live forever;
That the echoes of the words we speak,
Will resound until the end of time.

May our lives reflect this awareness;
May our deeds bring no shame or reproach.
May the entries we make
in the Book of Remembrance
Be ever acceptable to You.

Cantor Mitchell Kowitz

***

THE SOUL

How is it possible that this culture-loving era could be so monstrously
amoral?
More and more I come to value charity and love of one's fellow being
above everything else.
All our lauded technological progress - our very civilization -
is like the ax in the hand of a pathological criminal.

It is only to the individual that a soul is given.

The most beautiful experience we can have is the mysterious.
It is the fundamental emotion which stands
at the cradle of true art and true science....
I am satisfied with the mystery of the eternity of life.

*Small is the number of them that see with their own eyes
and feel with their own hearts.*

A hundred times every day I remind myself
that my inner and outer lives are based on the labors of other people,
living and dead, and that I must exert myself
in order to give in the same measure as I have received
and am still receiving.

*There is...something eternal that lies beyond reach
of the hand of fate and of all human delusions.
And such eternals lie closer to an older person....*

One misses the elementary reaction against injustice and for justice -
that reaction which in the long run represents our only protection
against a relapse into barbarism.

*The ancients knew something which we seem to have forgotten.
All means prove but a blunt instrument, if they have not behind them a
living spirit.*

Perfection of means and confusion of goals seem to characterize our
age.

*It is a mistake often made in this country to measure things by the amount
of money they cost.*

The most important human endeavor is the striving for morality in our
actions.
Our inner balance and even our very existence depend on it.
Only morality in our actions can give beauty and dignity to life.

Albert Einstein

***

ONLY THAT DAY DAWNS TO WHICH WE ARE AWAKE

I went to the woods because I wish to live deliberately, to front only the essential facts of life, and see if I could not learn what it had to teach, and not, when I came to die, to discover that I had not lived.

I did not wish to live what was not a life, living is so dear. Nor did I wish to practice resignation.... I wanted to live deep and suck out all the marrow of life, to live so sturdily and Spartan-like as to put to rout all that was not life, to cut a broad swath and shave close, to drive life into a corner, and reduce it to its lowest terms,

And, if it proved to be mean, why then to get the whole and genuine meanness out of it, and publish its meanness to the world; or if it were sublime, to know it by experience, and be able to give a true account of it....

Why should we live with such hurry and waste of life? ...When we are unhurried and wise, we perceive that only great and worthy things have any permanent and absolute existence, that petty fears and petty pleasures are but the shadow of the reality.

A man is rich in proportion to the number of things he can do without. Beware of all enterprises that require new clothes.

Public opinion is a weak tyrant compared with our own private opinion. What a man thinks of himself, that it is which determines, or rather indicates, his fate.

Only that day dawns to which we are awake.

Every man is the builder of a temple, called his body... We are all sculptors and painters, and our material is our own flesh and blood and bones. Any nobleness begins at once to refine a man's features, any meanness or sensuality to imbrute them.

Be not simply good; be good for something.

In the long run, men hit only what they aim at. Therefore...they had better aim at something high.

I know of no more encouraging fact than the unquestionable ability of man to elevate his life by conscious endeavor.

I learned this, at least, by my experiment: that if one advances confidently in the direction of his dreams, and endeavors to live the life which he had imagined, he will meet with a success unexpected in common hours.

Henry David Thoreau, *Walden*

***

TESHUVAH

THE SEVEN PATHS TO REPENTANCE

First: One must know that all will give account for wrong-doing.
If one does not repent God will demand an explanation of evil actions.

Second: One must know that there is great benefit to be derived from genuine repentance.

Third: One must try to understand the evil of our deeds
and why God is angered by them.
Unless one appreciates the nature of a sin, one cannot really change.

*Fourth: One must believe that all our evil ways are recorded,
that God knows all our deeds and nothing we do is unnoticed.*

Fifth: One must know that even many sins can be forgiven with
Teshuvah, for it is written (Ezekiel 33:12): "As for the wickedness of the
wicked, one shall not stumble thereby when one turns away from
wickedness."

*Sixth: One must reflect on God's kindness in dealing with humans.
God gave us an understanding heart, eyes to see, ears to hear, and a
body to serve the Almighty.*

Yet we pervert our own powers and mislead others, sinning with our body
and repaying God with evil for the goodness God gave us. As the Torah
says (Deuteronomy 32:6): "Do you thus requite Adonai, foolish people?"

*Seventh: One must recognize that it is not easy to repent and turn from
habit. One must battle and defeat the inclination which diverts a person
from the good path.*

There is a great reward for the one who masters the impulse to do wrong.
A repentant person must be disciplined and resist temptation.

*It is wise to stress the other extreme of one's passion, and so strive to
resist the attractive but harmful deed. Evil behavior is the greatest illness,
and only one who turns away from it is truly healthy.*

Menorat HaMaor -Yisrael ben Yosef al-Nakawa, (d. 1391, Spain)

"IT ALL DEPENDS ON ME!"

The following story is found in the Talmud. Once there was a man named Eliezer Ben Durdaya. He came from a fine background and a great future was predicted for him. However, he strayed from the path of Jewish life. He became addicted to the allurements of lust and passion and lived a sinful life.

One day, he heard a voice from heaven (his conscience, if you will) tell him, "Eliezer Ben Durdaya, you have no share in the world to come." He was moved to repentance, it was Rosh Hashanah, and he cried out these strange words. "Harim bakshu alai rahamim - O You majestic mountains, plead for me." When they refused he said, "Shemesh v'yareah - sun and moon, plead for me." But they also turned him down. He then exclaimed, "Kohavim u-mazalot - stars and planets, plead for me." And they, too, refused.

Finally Eliezer sat down and, after much soul-searching, he melted in tears and said, "Ein hadavar talu elah bi - it all depends on me." With that, another voice from heaven proclaimed, "M'zuman hu l'haye olam ha-ba - he is now ready to take his place in the world to come."

Rabbi Mitchel Wohlberg

***

THE THRONE OF GLORY

Rabbi Levi said: "Great is Teshuvah, for it reaches up to the Throne of Glory, as it is said: 'Return, O Israel, to Adonai your God.' "
Talmud, Tractate Yoma 86a

***

Every being that lives, grows.
Each will grow despite harsh
conditions and beautify its surroundings.

Like a tundra bloom,
the most striking and beautiful flower
is the one that blossoms
despite frigid, brutal conditions.

Judith Garrett Garrison and Scott Sheperd

***

NEW-CREATED

And if tonight my soul may find her peace
in sleep, and sink in good oblivion,
and in the morning wake like a
new-opened flower
then I have been dipped again in God,
and new-created.

D.H. Lawrence

***

NUMBER MY DAYS THIS WAY

O Lord-
Number my days this way:

Days of strength to lie,
if the truth brings torment.
Days of weakness,
if strength gives rise to suffering.
Days of noise,
if silence is the cause of loneliness.
And
Nights of disconcerting dreams
if I turn smug to the taste of hunger.

Pursue me,
Discomfort me,
Destroy my own complacency
with paradox and contradiction.

Remind me I am Yours.

Danny Siegel

***

If you're not working on yourself you're not working

TESHUVAH

One of the most important and original terms of Jewish moral thought, *teshuvah* is quite inadequately rendered by the usual translation "repentance." To repent is to turn away from sin and seek forgiveness. *Teshuvah* is a broader concept, one that goes to the very root of human existence. It is no wonder that the *Talmud* lists the power of *teshuvah* as one of those seven things that existed before God created this world. Human life is inconceivable without *teshuvah*.

The first person to undertake *teshuvah* was the very first human. Adam realized the magnitude of his sin in the Garden, according to the *Midrash*, and sought to be reconciled with God. *Teshuvah* in this case would mean re-establishing the intimacy and trust that existed between God and God's beloved creatures before the expulsion from Eden. *Teshuvah*, in this key story, could not mean the re-creation of innocence. That childlike aspect of Eden was gone forever. But a new relationship, one more mature since it had faced and overcome the moment of doubt and betrayal, was Adam's goal. It is this deeper faith, one that emerges from struggle with the self, that is the goal of *teshuvah*.

Another great paradigm of *teshuvah* is the Biblical tale of Jonah. For this reason it is read in the synagogue on Yom Kippur afternoon, as the special season of *teshuvah* draws near to its close. God teaches the prophet Jonah not to be cynical, to always maintain faith in the possibility of human transformation, just as God does. The prophet, who had longed for God to destroy the wicked city of Nineveh, is reminded that the city contains "more than a hundred and twenty thousand people who do not know their right hand from their left, and much cattle" (Jonah 4: 11). Most sinners are like fools or children, not knowing right from left, no more guilty than cattle. Their Creator does not want to destroy them, but to see them transform their lives by turning to God.

The *Kabbalah* views *teshuvah* as a cosmic process, one that extends beyond humans and encompasses all life and being. It is identified with *binah*, the third of the ten *sefirot* and the maternal force within God. All creatures are derived from the divine womb, and all contain within them a deep longing to return to that source. The human desire to reach out to God is as whole and natural as the tree's stretching to grow toward the sunlight or the root's sinking deeper into the earth in quest for water.

Rabbi Arthur Green

***

THE STATE OF ISRAEL

THE MIRACLE OF SPIRITUAL REBIRTH

Each of us at times feels
Defeated...Discouraged...Tired of life,
Numb, dead to the world, An old bag of bones

Even a society, an entire people
goes through periods of such despair.
At such time we need to remind ourselves
of God's word to the biblical prophet Ezekiel:

"The hand of the Lord was on me...
And set me down in the midst of a valley
filled with bones... very many and very dry.
God said: 'O mortal, can these bones live?'

I answered 'only God knows.'
God said, 'Prophesy about these bones thus:
"Behold I will cause breath to enter you and you shall live...." '
So I prophesied as he commanded me,
and spirit came into them and they lived.'
Then God said to me: 'these bones are the whole house of Israel
who say:

"Our bones are dried, Our hopes are lost, We are cut off."
But I shall put my spirit in you and you shall live.' "

From death's despair, illnesses' pains
Separation's loneliness, failure's futility,
And depression's hopelessness;

We will be revived, Resurrecting our spirits,
Rebuilding our soul, Restoring our lives.

It has happened before, it will happen again
The miracle of spiritual rebirth.
We must believe in it. And when we do,
It will happen again for us...now.

Rabbi Allen S. Maller

***

TODAY - HA-YOM

Look to this day,
For it is life,
The very life of Life.

In its brief course lie all
The realities and verities of existence,

The bliss of growth,
The splendor of action,
The glory of power–

For yesterday is but a dream,
And tomorrow is only a vision,
But today, well lived,

Makes every yesterday a dream of happiness
And every tomorrow a vision of hope.

Sanskrit Prayer

***

Waking up this morning,
I smile.
Twenty-four brand new hours are before me.
I vow to live fully in each moment
and to look at all beings
with eyes of compassion.

Thich Nhat Hanh

***

Lord, for tomorrow and its needs, I do not pray;
But keep me, guide me, love me, Lord, just for today.

Anonymous

***

NOW

Source of our strength, Who gives meaning to our days and years and grants us shalom, Help us to understand that now is the best of times for **Shalom**.

Now is the best time to forgive - *Selihah*
Now is the best time to love - *Ahavah*

Now is the best time to be Jewish.
Now is the best time to work for *Shalom*.
Now is the best time to enjoy life - *L'Hayim*
Now is the best time to share - *Tzedakah*
Now is the best time to support Israel.
Now is the best time to be good Americans.
Now is the best time to make the most of life - To Be *Shalame* - whole.

Rabbi Bernard S. Raskas

***

Now is the time
To climb up the mountain
And reason against habit.
Now is the time.

Now is the time
To renew the barren soil of nature
Ruined by the winds of tyranny.
Now is the time.

Now is the time
To commence the litany of hope.
Now is the time.

Now is the time
To give me roses, not to keep them
For my grave to come.
Give them to me while my heart beats,
Give them today
While my heart yearns for jubilee.
Now is the time....

Mzwakhe Mbuli, activist, South Africa

***

JUST FOR TODAY

Just for today I will live one day only, forgetting yesterday and tomorrow, and not trying to solve the whole problem of life at once.

> *Just for today I will be unafraid of life and death; unafraid to enjoy the beautiful and to be happy.*

Just for today I will adjust myself to what is, and try not to make everything over to suit me. If I cannot have what I like, I will try to like what I have.

> *Just for today I will be agreeable, cheerful, charitable, do my best, praise people for what they do, not criticize them for what they cannot do; and if I find fault, I will forgive it and forget it. I will not try to improve or regulate anybody except myself.*

Just for today I will have a plan. I may not follow it exactly, but I will have one. It will save me from worry, hurry and indecision.

> *Just for today I will get people off my nerves and not get on theirs. I will appreciate them for what they do and what they are.*

Just for today I will not show it if my feelings are hurt.

> *Just for today I will find a little time for quiet, to relax, and to realize what life is and can be; time to think about God, and get a better perspective of myself.*

Just for today I will look at life with fresh eyes and discover the wonder of it; I will know that as I give to the world so the world will give to me.

Rabbi Bernard S. Raskas
(adapted from K.P.L. Magazine)

***

TORAH

YOUR TEACHINGS ARE MY MUSIC AND SONG

A Jew is a person in love with Torah.

A Jew says to God, with the Psalmist:
Make Your face shine upon Your servant.
Teach me Your commandments.

Open up my eyes and make me see the wonders of Torah.

Your kindness fills the Universe.
Fill me kindly with your teachings.

Your words, Lord, shall be a lamp to my feet, a light for my path.

Were not Your Torah to me a thing of joy,
I would have long perished from the earth.

I shall never forsake Your teachings.
Because of them I feel alive.

I love the Torah with all my might;
it is the constant talk of my days.

The Torah is to me much more precious
than endless silver and gold.

I rejoice over each new word, each new insight,
as if I had found a hidden fortune.

Your teachings are my music and song
wherever I go and wherever I live.

My soul will sing to You continually;
it will not be silent.

Rabbi Noah Golinkin

***

TRADITION

BY EXAMPLE AND DEED

From generation to generation the wisdom of living is handed down.

From parents to children, from grandparents to grandchildren.

Life's messages, both great and small, are carved deeply in our hearts.

Not by wonder alone but by the most ancient communication of all: love.

Love of truth and justice is handed down not by words alone.

But by example, deed and personal involvement.

Love of Judaism is not generated by teachings and exhortations alone.

But by being role models in observance, practice and participation.

Love for family is not based on verbal commands and spoken instructions.

But by affection, loyalty and warmth in demonstration and deeds.

We teach effectively not by what we say, but by what we are and do.

As we watch the flow of life, we learn the skill of living in God's good time.

Rabbi Bernard S. Raskas

***

WE ARE CLAY   (Kee Hinei KaHomer)

We are clay.
You are the Potter
Who shapes us at His will.
Mold us into worthy vessels
Even though we're only clay.
Do not smash us if we prove imperfect.
Remember we are only clay.

We are glass.
You are the craftsman
Who can blow us into many shapes.
Form us into finest crystal
Even if You have to twist and turn us.
But do not smash us if we are not pure.
Remember we are only glass.

We are silver.
You are the smith
Who molds us as He wishes.
Hammer us as You design
Even though we are not gold.
Do not smash us if we tarnish.
Remember we are only silver.

We are the rudder.
You are the helmsman
Who steers us to the left or to the right.
Direct us to the shore You choose.
Do not let us idly spin
Even if we constantly resist your grasp.
Remember that the waves are very strong.

We are threads.
You are the weaver
Who creates the patterns that he likes.
Weave us, God, into Your plan.
Make us supple, straight, and true.
And do not throw us in a heap
If we should not be perfect.
Remember we are only threads.

- Interpretative translation by Rabbi Michael Hecht -

109

YIZKOR

SPRING WILL COME

The wintry wind blows away the snow
And knocks on the mountain window.

The bitter draught on the door
Withers the sleeping plum-blossoms,

But however much it despoils the flower,
Can it prevent the spring coming?

Yun Sun-Do

***

Teach me your mood, o patient stars!
Who climb each night the ancient sky,
Leaving on space no shade, no scars,
No trace of age, no fear to die.

Ralph Waldo Emerson

***

YOU ARE A CONSOLATION
TO YOUR CREATURES

O Lord,
You are a consolation to Your creatures,
for in moments of forgetting,
we but call to mind Your care,
and we are comforted.

When we hope no more,
a pattern in the snow
reminds us of Your lovingkindness.

Your dawns give us confidence, and sleep is a friend,
Our sorrows dissipate
in the presence of an infant's smile,
and the wise words of the old
revive our will-to-wish.

Your hints are everywhere,
Your signals in the most remote of places.

You are here,
and we fail words to say,
"Mah Tov!"
How good our breath,
our rushing energies,
our silences of love.

Danny Siegel

***

GOD, MAKE ME BRAVE FOR LIFE

God, make me brave for life; oh, braver than this.
Let me straighten after pain, as a tree straightens after the rain,
Shining and lovely again.
God, make me brave for life, much braver than this.
As the blown grass lifts, let me rise from sorrow with quiet eyes,
Knowing Your way is wise.
God, make me brave, life brings such blinding things.
Help me to keep my sight; Help me to see aright
That out of dark comes light.

Anonymous

AN ETHICAL WILL FROM MOTHER TO DAUGHTER

Dearest Sarah, will you laugh if I tell you that the mind picture of the future I most cherish is of you studying Torah with those children to be? It sounds so corny, and we both remember the hours we spent together during your day school years pouring over Hebrew texts, your homework assignments. I would get impatient (can you ever forgive the impatience?) and you frustrated, with the amount of study time your demanding schedule required. Grandpa had studied with me the same way when I was young. Dare you repeat such family patterns with your own children?

I think you will. I think you must. From those hours and years of study grew your own love of Torah and your delight in chanting from the Torah scrolls. There grew also, I believe, even with the impatience and frustrations, a bond between us linked inseparably in some mysterious way to the tradition and the texts we studied together, and that too, is sacred.

These days, women (you and I among them), increasingly question the text and traditions to which we have devoted so much energy. You know the problems well; the relentless maleness in our religion, the silences that surround the birth, thoughts and feelings of women in sacred texts, the sense of exclusion we so often experience even today. It is terribly important for you to hold those issues in your mind so that you might apply your own skills toward working with other caring women and men committed to bringing about change.

But I hope you will never fall into the trap of thinking that because some things are wrong, everything is wrong. I hope that the very process of questioning and creating change will lead not to rejection but to a deeper love and more profound understanding of our tradition, to a greater desire than ever to be fully included within it.

As for the Scriptures, even if they sometimes pain us, they are the heartblood of all that we hold dear as Jews. They form the core of our history and values, our myths and love stories, our sociology, our legal doctrines, our soul as people. Know them, Sarah. Teach them to your children, yes, one on one, as Grandpa taught me and I taught you. Without knowledge of our texts, whatever else they know of Judaism will be insufficient. With that knowledge, they will know how to learn everything else.

On Yom Kippur this year, just two weeks before your birthday, I listened with pride, as I always do, while you chanted the book of Jonah, the annual reading you have taken on since your Bat Mitzvah. But this year, I swallowed tears as I watched you, wrapped in your prayer shawl, standing tall and confident, singing out the familiar Hebrew words in your lovely, strong voice.

Francine Klagsburn

112

Jacob the Baker

by Noah benShea

"Jacob, where do you find the strength to carry on in life?"

"Life is often heavy only because we attempt to carry it," said Jacob. "But, I do find a strength in the ashes'"

"In the ashes?" asked Mr. Gold.

"Yes," said Jacob, with a confirmation that seemed to have traveled a great distance.

"You see, Mr. Gold, each of us is alone. Each of us is in the great darkness of our ignorance. And, each of us is on a journey.

"In the process of our journey, we must bend to build a fire for light, and warmth, and food.

"But when our fingers tear at the ground, hoping to find the coals of another's fire, what we often find are the ashes.

"And, in these ashes, which will not give us light or warmth, there may be sadness, but there is also testimony.   I

"Because these ashes tell us that somebody else has been in the night, somebody else has bent to build a fire, and somebody else has carried on.

"And that can be enough, sometimes."

***

A REFLECTION ON DEATH

If life is a pilgrimage, death is an arrival, a celebration.
The last words should be neither craving nor bitterness,
but peace and gratitude.
We have been given so much. Why is the outcome of our lives so little?

*Our embarrassment is like an abyss. Whatever we give away is so much
less than what we receive. Perhaps this is the meaning of dying:
to give one's whole self away.*

Unless we cultivate sensitivity to the Glory while we are here,
unless we learn how to experience a foretaste of heaven while on earth,
what can there be in store for us in life to come?

*The seed of eternal life is planted within us here and now.
But a seed is wasted when placed on stone,
into souls that die while the body is still alive.*

The greatest problem is not how to continue our lives
but how to exalt our existence.

*The cry for a life beyond the grave is presumptuous
if there is no cry for eternal life prior to our descent into the grave.*

Our greatest problem is not how to continue but how to return.
"How can I pray unto the Lord
in all God's bountiful dealings with me," Psalm 116:12 asks.

When life is an answer, death is a homecoming.

This is the meaning of existence,
to reconcile liberty with service, the passing with the lasting,
to weave the threads of temporality into the fabric of eternity.

*This is the meaning of Death,
the ultimate self-dedication to the Divine.*

Death so understood will not be distorted by the craving of immortality:
for this act of "giving away"
is reciprocity on our part of God's gift of life.
For the pious human, it is a privilege to die.

Rabbi Abraham Joshua Heschel

***

ACKNOWLEDGEMENTS

Special appreciation is offered to several colleagues who helped in various stages of this collection, through moral support, advice, help in selection of material, reading various drafts of the manuscript, and other ways. These include Rabbis Stephen Chaim Listfield, Bruce Dollin, Sylvan Kamens, Michael Hecht, Jonathan Ginsburg, Noah Golinkin, Kenneth L. Cohen, Harold Kushner, Shafrir Lev, Allen S. Maller, and Dr. Shoshana Silberman.

No parts of this collection may be reprinted or reproduced in any media without written permission from the copyright holder. All attempts have been made to obtain permission from holders of copyrights from authors and publications included. Any oversight in this regard will be corrected should a second printing be warranted, and apologies are offered to anyone regarding any possible errors. Please communicate any matters to this subject to the editor at the address on the title page.

Grateful acknowledgment is offered to those rabbis, authors, editors and publishers, who graciously granted permission to use their material for this collection. These include Rabbis Isaiah Zeldin (Stephen S. Wise Synagogue, Los Angeles), Sylvan Kamens, Michael Hecht, Daniel A. Jezer, Sandy Eisenberg Sasso, Henry Cohen, Michael Lerner, Rami Shapiro, Jack Riemer, Lawrence Kushner, Zelig Piskin, Chaim Stern, Bernard S. Raskas, Zalman Schachter-Shalomi, Sheldon Zimmerman, Julie K. Gordon, Jonathan Ginsburg, Dov Peretz Elkins, Allen S. Maller, Mitchell Wohlberg, Arthur Green. I want to express my deepest gratitude to Maxine Elkins whose artistic eye helped make the appearance of the book as attractive as it is. Special thanks to Janice Berg for her assistance with this manuscript.

C. Douglas Ballon, Cantor Mitchell Kowitz, excerpts from Ruth F. Brin, Harvest: Collected Poems and Prayers (Reconstructionist Press, 1986, reprinted by permission of Ruth F. Brin; Danny Siegel, TIKKUN Magazine: A bimonthly Jewish Critique of Politics, Culture and Society (Subscriptions $29 from TIKKUN, 951 Cragmont Ave., Berkeley, CA 94708); Yitzhak Buxbaum, Belleruth Naparstek; Alicia Ostriker, "A Prayer to the Shkhina," by Alicia Ostriker, © Alicia Ostriker, contributed by the author - from